The
Jasper's
Cookbook

The *Jasper's* Cookbook

Celebrating 50 Years of Recipes from Kansas City's Legendary Restaurant

by

Jasper J. Mirabile, Jr.

Back cover photo by Greg Gorman
Illustrations by Dan Robeson
Chef Portrait by Greg Gorman

ISBN: 1-58597-194-4

Library of Congress Control Number: 2003111768

A division of Squire Publishers, Inc.
4500 College Blvd.
Leawood, KS 66211
888-888-7696
www.leatherspublishing.com

To my mother and father —

who encouraged and inspired me,

who gave me opportunity and knowledge,

and whose legacy lives on every day.

Acknowledgments

To my wife, Lisa, and daughter, Alexandra, who listen to my rants and raves, critique my cooking, and make life worth living.

To my brother, Leonard, who runs our business and watches everything from behind the scenes, never getting credit, and who has to read my handwriting, as bad as it is.

To my brother, Salvatore, my chief taster and attorney, who loves my food and thinks he can run a computer.

To my brother, James (who thinks he can run a restaurant), my personal doctor, to whom I also go for advice. I can feed you anything and you are always satisfied.

To my sisters-in-law — Janine, Marla and Vicki — who put up with the "Mirabile Boys" in good times and in bad, who love to travel, and who are just like the sisters I never had.

To my nephew and nieces — Jasper III, JoMarie, Christina, Jovana and Nicole — who grew up thinking I was their cousin, not their uncle; who share my days off; and who still, to this day, ask Uncle Jay to cook their favorite dishes.

To my friend, Greg Gorman, for whom I enjoy cooking every time he visits Kansas City. Thank you for your photographs and friendship.

To my mother and father-in-law, Margaret and Reg, for your support, praise and understanding of my cooking.

To Linda Davis, for believing in me and giving me opportunity.

To Laura O'Rourke and the staff at the Culinary Center of Kansas City, for all your help with my recipes and the opportunity to use your venue for my classes.

To all my friends at Gruppo Ristoratori Italiani, DiRoNA and Slow Food USA.

To Tom Leathers and his staff, for working with me, editing and publishing my recipes.

To my dear friend, Anna Amendolara Nurse, for taking all my calls, my Beard House dinners, and for sharing with me all her love. Mille Grazie!

To Tony May and Roberto Donna for letting me share your experiences in Italy and with GRI.

To Tony Civella, for your guidance, support and love.

To my G.M., Sam Gianino — your many hours of hard work and respect for my family are appreciated.

To Marvin Lewis, my assistant and chef for 28 years, always behind me 100%. To my staff, who put up with me every day, who cover for my mistakes, and who work 15-hour days; and to my assistants, who know my recipes by heart, and who watch my place as if it is their own — I thank you the most for keeping my father's legacy alive today.

To my suppliers, who get my daily phone messages and e-mail. How you put up with my critique of your products, I do not know. You are all the best and keep me on top.

To my critics, who I have all told to walk one day in my shoes before you review my restaurant or cookbook — you have been fair and honest, always praising Jasper's with rave reviews.

To Betty Martin and her late husband, Roy, who keep me supplied with chocolate.

To Joey and Gerry Corkle, my dear friends, for your support and inspiration while writing this cookbook.

To Vivien Jennings and Roger Doran from Rainy Day Books in Fairway, Kansas — you have given me guidance and support, and I can never stop thanking you.

To Karen Adler, for all your advice.

To my customers — you are so loyal. For over 50 years, you have been coming to my family's establishment.

And, finally, to all who dined at Jasper's for special occasions — prom nights, engagements, first restaurant experiences, etc. — I thank each and every one of you.

Contents

Precoce

This story began over a century ago when my grandfather, Leonardo Mirabile, immigrated from Sicily to find a new beginning in America.

My father, Jasper, learned to cook from his mother, my Nana, Josephine. When he was eight years old, my father would cook pasta at home after school and place it in a basket on his bicycle and ride to the family grocery store in New Jersey to bring dinner to his mom and pop. He played football in high school and college at St. Mary's in California, but he eventually came back home to Kansas City. There he met my mother, Josephine, and together with his parents they purchased a small bar named Roses at 75th and Wornall in Waldo in south Kansas City. His critics said he would never make it "way out there." It was the county line, the end of the old streetcar line, just way too far out.

He used recipes from my Nana and began his restaurant. He didn't have the knowledge of accounting, staffing or running a business. What he did have was a dream. He had a dream to run the best restaurant in the city and offer authentic Italian food to Kansas City. Everyone agrees he reached his dream, especially when he was inducted in 1996 into the Distinguished Restaurants of North America (DiRoNa) "Hall of Fame," over forty years after opening Jasper's on April Fool's Day in 1954.

Many people do not know how he struggled, not even having enough money for a lock on his apartment door, or how my mom would take his suit to the cleaners every morning, the same suit because he could not afford to buy another one. He would tell me stories of how the first year in business he would do $1,200 a week in sales, about $60,000 that first year, but he never gave up. He always strived to be better and offer his guests something they never had tasted before. Over the years and many remodelings later, he began to add new dishes to the menu. The three most important, Scampi ala Livornese, Capellini D' Angelo and Veal Lemonata Dore. He treasured these dishes and would only teach his chef, Manual Cervantes, the recipes.

Many restaurants have tried to copy these dishes, but only Jasper had the original recipe for our "signature" dishes still on the menu today. Business began to grow in the 1960s, and my parents began to live their dream, purchasing the original building and expanding the restaurant.

Finally, in 1972, Holiday Magazine Awards honored Jasper's as one of the top 100 restaurants in America. Mobil 4 Stars, Cartier Gold Plate, AAA 4 Diamonds and many other awards soon followed. Rave reviews in *The Kansas City Star, Gourmet Magazine* and *Bon Appetit* all did the same. During this time, my mother and father began to travel, going to New York, San Francisco, Rome, Florence, Milan and Paris, always bringing back new recipes and more ideas. He would add new dining rooms with Murano glass chandeliers from Venice, Fortuni fabrics from Milan, Axminster carpeting from England, along with fine white tablecloths, fine china and tuxedoed waiters.

Jasper's was "the place to dine when in Kansas City," as *Time Magazine* reported in 1976 during the Republican Convention. There wasn't a night in the dining room that you would not find my father making his famous Caesar Salad, tossing Pasta Carbonara or flaming a Kansas City Peppered Steak tableside. Special guests would be able to enjoy Crepes Gran Vefore or Cherries Jubilee.

Things pretty much stayed the same at Jasper's, with my dad running the business, until my brother Leonard joined him in 1975 after my grandfather passed away. Leonard began to run the daily operations, and in 1984 I joined him and my father full-time. We opened a small Italian market named Marco Polo's. An authentic trattoria followed, as did an Old World coffee shop, "Il Caffe." We worked together for thirteen years, constantly updating our menu, adding more wines, creating new dishes and offering the Midwest a world class operation.

In 1997, after many months of negotiations, we sold our property and buildings at 75th Street that we had purchased over the years to Walgreen's Drugstore. We set up our offices at 103rd Street and State Line in Watts Mill Shopping Center. We began to build our new restaurant, a casual yet elegant Italian restaurant and unique Italian market and deli. Our new restaurant was under construction for fifteen months when my father passed away. Gone was an era in Kansas City of one of the most noted restaurateurs in the country. Now it was time for Leonard and me to carry on the tradition. Sixty days later we opened the new Jasper's Italian Restaurant and Marco Polo's Deli to rave reviews and larger crowds of customers that had waited nearly eighteen months for us to reopen.

The most common question I hear today is, "How old were you when you started cooking?" To answer that, I remember when I was three years old helping (or pestering) my mom and Nana in the family kitchen on Sundays. Everything in our life always centered around food. It was so interesting as a child to open a refrigerator, put ingredients in a bowl and after awhile taste your creation. I can remember my Nana making her famous rum cake and boiling the oranges and lemons in simple syrup and rum that would later soak the fresh-baked sponge cake. I can still see the "babbaluci" (fresh snails) crawling out of the pot when she would make her special dinner for family visiting from Sicily. I watched with excitement when my mom would fill 150 cream puffs for a holiday dessert or roll 75-100 meatballs for our Sunday dinners.

Nothing influenced me more than the first time I really walked into my father's kitchen on 75th Street. Everything looked so big, the stoves and ovens, even the plates. When most kids were out playing T-ball in the summer, I would sit on the big chopping block in Jasper's kitchen and watch the cooks prepare lunch orders. My dad's chef, Manual, would always let me stir something, whether it was Cannoli filling, which I should have been folding, or mixing in the eggs to his custard. I would spend hours making mental notes, observing the cooks making sauces, reducing stocks, grilling meats, pounding out veal and sautéing vegetables. I was too young to work at nights, so I would go home and play with my friends, yet always calling my dad to ask what he was doing or what was he eating, ending every conversation with, "Are you going to be late? Can I work Saturday night with my brothers?" I finally got my first chance to work, following my three older brothers' footsteps cutting the bread. My first real job was to slice the bread and make up baskets for bus help to bring to the guests' tables. Too easy. I lasted about a month. I wanted to work the salad station.

As fate and luck would have it, one salad lady was sick one night, and I was allowed to help the other salad lady. Did I love it! A dream come true. Now I did the salad job for about a year every Friday and Saturday nights. I learned to chop onions and cucumbers, slice tomatoes, mushrooms and carrots. I cut lettuce and tore the Romaine, picked the spinach and learned to make croutons. I learned every salad dressing recipe, even adding my own two cents, adjusting the Italian Dressing with more sugar and adding more Romano cheese to the Creamy Italian Dressing.

My dad had a small window from the kitchen to his office back then, and I would constantly communicate with him. On Saturdays he would "work the wheel," calling in orders to the cooks, setting up the carts going out to the dining room, yet all the while keeping his watchful eye on me. He would tell his cooks, "Teach Jay how to make the tomato sauce today," or "Show Jay how I want that plate to look." I decided that someday I would be a chef, creating dishes and making people happy. As I grew older, maybe nine or ten, I began to work on the appetizer station, making dishes of babbaluci, eggplant and shrimp cocktail. This is also when I first learned the secrets to Scampi ala Livornese, a recipe I have treasured and kept a secret to this day.

When I was twelve, I began to watch the "big cooks" sauté veal, chicken and seafood. I learned to trim a whole tenderloin of beef, cut racks of lamb and break down a whole leg of veal. I also learned the trick of boning fresh fish, shucking oysters, clams and mussels. I began my first real on-the-line training when I was thirteen, cooking on the pasta station and finally the end of the line, the grill. For some unknown reason, I had to be like my brothers; I wanted to work in the dining room. I was fourteen and in the eighth grade. I pleaded with my dad to make me a bus boy. I wanted to wear a tuxedo. My mom and I put one together from my brothers' hand-me-downs. My first night, I was all dressed and ready to work, and Roy, the maitre d', gave me my first black bow tie. I was now a bus boy.

I really liked it out front at first, cleaning tables, getting bread and butter, water, and just running through the dining room cleaning ashtrays and picking up dirty plates, assisting the waiters and captains. This is when I found my fondness for talking to customers, meeting celebrities, sports players, owners of large corporations, actors and actresses. I was enthralled by our dessert cart shown to every table, with the servers describing each house-made dessert. I wanted to show the cart myself, so I followed our head captain one evening, making notes of his descriptions to the customers. I then went one step further, talking to the pastry chef for his inside information about how they did the desserts to make them so special. Now I was ready to show the cart. The first time I had the chance, I showed it to a party of six guests. I described everything perfectly and even added my own touch, "The chocolate cake is very good, my mom makes it." I successfully sold all six people desserts. A few months later, a cookbook was written by the noted Los Angeles restaurant critic and founder of the Travel Holiday Award, Robert Lawrence Balzer. A feature article was written about Jasper's of Kansas City, and Mr. Balzer spoke of Jasper's youngest son, Jasper Jr., who showed the dessert cart. He was so impressed by the dessert cart, he wanted one of each. Who knew that first evening I was waiting on this distinguished gentleman? The dessert cart is still shown to every guest in our dining room.

That same year was the first time my parents took me to Italy. What a vacation — dining in the finest restaurants in Rome, Milan, Florence, Naples, Sorrento, Calabria, and finally a week with my grandfather in his hometown of Gibelina, Sicily, eating with cousins I had never met, discovering for the first time Sicilian blood oranges, arancine, pasta con sarde, and my cousins' gelato and granita, and touring the famous Vucciria, Palermo's outdoor market. I followed my father's lead and took notes of every dish I ate and discovered, describing the presentation and taste. To this day, I still record every dinner when traveling outside Kansas City, seeking new dishes, wines and food products to bring back to our restaurant, always remembering how my father taught me.

Every summer during my high school years, I would travel to Italy, touring wineries with the famous owners, and dining at restaurants where I was greeted with open arms like a family member returning home after a long journey. I attended cooking classes the following summers in Paris, Florence and Venice, filling notepads that I still use today to create dishes for the restaurant and cooking classes.

My first cooking class was in 1983, and I taught it at the old Wolferman's in Fairway. Linda Davis gave me my first opportunity to showcase my family's restaurant and my cooking talent. In that first class I demonstrated Caesar salad, Fettucini Alfredo, Veal Limonata and Canolli Gelato. In 1984, I began teaching classes at our restaurant — 45-50 people every two weeks for 14 years, teaching friends, family and customers our recipes of regional Italian dishes.

To this day, I read every food publication I can get my hands on and have collected over 2,500 cookbooks that I use for research and personal use. I travel to Italy often, sometimes twice a year, visiting different regions and attending cooking classes. I love the culture, the food, the people and, most of all, appreciation of my heritage.

Today, I am actively involved with the American Institute of Wine and Food as co-chairman of the Kansas City chapter, board member of Gruppo Ristauratori Italian (GRI) and founding leader and director of Slow Food Kansas City. I teach classes every month at the Culinary Center of Kansas City and hold monthly seminars on food and wine at Jasper's. I consult for many national and international companies and enjoy helping and creating recipes and menus for my many friends and colleges in the restaurant industry. I can be found cooking nightly at the restaurant, upholding a tradition that was started over 50 years ago.

Our restaurant and market now seat over 300 guests in a casual but elegant atmosphere, offering diners a patio view of Indian Creek, a menu that includes Old World dishes and new plates of pasta, veal, chicken, seafood and chops. Enoteca da Jasper features an authentic Italian wine bar and cellar room with over 400 different wines. Our deli, market and pizzeria is in front of our restaurant and offers grilled Italian sausages off a cart streetside. We now employ over 50 people who are dedicated to cooking, serving and satisfying the thousands of guests who dine at our restaurant.

A Family and Its History ... in Pictures

Mirabile family wedding, circa 1927.

My father and Papa Mirabile at Ellis Island.

Great-grandfather Jasper Mirabile, circa 1920.

Left: Jasper Mirabile, Sr. in 1942.

Right: Josephine (Nana) Mirabile, 1942.

A family trip to Sicily, 1938.

Leonard, Jasper, Jr., James and Salvatore.
(Seated) Jasper, Sr. — 1976.

Grandpa Mirabile and his bakery — 1930.

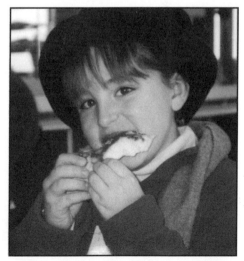

Jasper, Sr. — 1938.

Jasper, Sr. as a student at DeLaSalle Academy — 1944.

Alexandra Mirabile — 2001.

Jasper, Jr. and Jasper, Sr. at the first dinner at the James Beard House — 1995.

The Gibellina flag.

Left: Jasper, Jr. in 1980.

Right: Papa Leonardo's home in Gibellina, Sicily — 1962.

Antipasti

Antipasti

Every Italian meal begins with a "starter." In Sicily, my family calls it *"grape u pitittu,"* which means "mouth openers." This could be small plates of olives, salami, prosciutto, assorted cheeses or a variety of cold vegetables simply dressed with olive oil.

It is my personal experience to always judge a good restaurant or chef by his antipasti, giving me a preview of his coming dishes.

When I plan a menu for customers or personal friends and family, I always try to serve something exciting to start the dinner. I can usually make a meal just with antipasti, a loaf of bread and some Proseco.

A true Italian table contains many plates of antipasti, encouraging guests to share and enjoy.

Stuffed Peppers Angelo

1/4 C.	olive oil
1	large eggplant cubed
1/2	onion julienne
1	can tomatoes, 15 oz., chopped
3	cloves chopped garlic
1/4 tsp.	dried basil
1/2 tsp.	sugar
1/2 tsp.	salt
	black pepper, to taste
4	chopped anchovies
18	fresh black olives, cut and halved
5	large mushrooms, sliced
3 Tbs.	capers
3 C.	croutons, plain
2 Tbs.	cream sherry
1/4	cup raisins
6	green bell peppers, cut and halved (par-boiled 10 minutes)
2 C.	Marinara sauce *(Recipe on page 43)*

Sauté eggplant and onion slowly in 1/4 C. olive oil. Add tomatoes, chopped garlic, basil, sugar, salt and pepper. Sauté until onion is opaque. Add chopped anchovies; stir, add black olives. Cook about 5 minutes over medium heat. Add mushrooms and capers. Sauté for 2-3 minutes.

Add croutons, stir well. Add cream sherry. Stir and let croutons soak up all sauce. Add raisins. Mix well and stuff each pepper half. Roast on a cookie sheet in oven at 350° for 35 minutes, or until peppers are tender. Don't overcook or peppers will get mushy. Leave kind of hard. Top each pepper with hot Marinara sauce and serve.

Serves 8-10.

The first restaurant that I dined in while visiting New York City was Angelo's on Mulberry St. Ironically, this is the first place my father was taken to by my grandfather. I love the stuffed peppers, linguini with fresh clams, and all the veal dishes at Angelo's. My father worked on this recipe many times, adding anchovies, less croutons, and tomatoes, until he was satisfied with the dish. Whenever I visit New York as a guest chef or for pleasure, I always head straight down to "Little Italy" at Mulberry and Grand and enjoy my dinner at Angelo's.

Parma Cream

2 Tbs. grated Parmigiano Reggiano
cheese
2 avocados
2 Tbs. extra virgin olive oil
2 Tbs. fresh lemon juice
2 Tbs. whipped cream
pinch salt
pinch pepper
4 avocados, peeled and sliced
4 oz. sliced Prosciutto di Parma

Peel, pit and slice two avocados. Place in food processor and add olive oil, Parmigiano Reggiano, lemon juice, whipped cream, salt and pepper. Mix thoroughly. Arrange on a serving dish with avocado slices and Prosciutto di Parma. Serve with lightly toasted foccacia or crostini.

Serves 4-6.

 This is such a simple dish, but so flavorful. I usually let this sit refrigerated for 6 hours, place in a pastry bag and pipe onto crostini with various salami. This also is great on a panini with melted provolone. I try to use a Sicilian extra virgin olive oil; they usually are very fruity and give a great olive taste to my cooking.

Steamed Mussels

3 doz.	cleaned and scrubbed mussels
1-1/2 tsp.	minced garlic
3 Tbs.	olive oil
3-4	fresh Roma tomatoes, peeled and chopped
1 tsp.	oregano
1 Tbs.	butter
3/4 C.	dry white wine
2 Tbs.	minced parsley
1/4 tsp.	red pepper flakes
1 C.	clam juice

Heat olive oil in a 2-quart deep sauce pan. Add mussels and tomatoes. Cook 3-4 minutes. Add garlic; remove from heat. Let stand 2-3 minutes. Place back on heat, reduce pan with wine, add parsley, butter, oregano and red pepper flakes. Cook 2-3 more minutes. Add 1/2 cup clam juice and reduce 1 more minute. Place in large serving bowl and serve hot.

Serves 3-4.

This is really a quick appetizer and makes an intense broth. The best way to serve this dish is with a thick piece of crusty garlic toast. My grandmother would cook babbalucci (small snails) in this same cooking method. I feel the seasoning blend of oregano, parsley and red pepper flakes makes this dish appealing. When I want to make this a meal in itself, I add 1/4 cup of pastina (peppercorn size pasta) to the broth and let this cook 10 minutes before adding the mussels.

Sicilian Caponatina

3	whole eggplants
3	stalks celery
1/2	onion
1/2 C.	olive oil
10	whole green olives, sliced
3 tsp.	capers
12 oz.	tomato sauce
2 Tbs.	red wine vinegar
1/2 C.	raisins
2 Tbs.	sugar
1 tsp.	chopped parsley
1 tsp.	salt
1/4 tsp.	red pepper flakes
	crostini

Peel eggplant and chop into 1/2" cubes. Dice celery and onions. In a large skillet, heat olive oil. Add eggplant, celery and onions. Cook 12-15 minutes over medium heat. Add olives, capers, tomato sauce, vinegar, raisins, sugar, parsley, salt and red pepper flakes. Stir thoroughly and remove from heat. Cool in refrigerator for 1 hour. Serve chilled with crostini.

Serves 6-8.

 Caponatina is a true Sicilian dish, served chilled on an antipasti table. I always serve this dish to my friends before some of my big dinners. I have even warmed the caponata and used it as a bed for roasted sea bass or tuna. This dish is one of the oldest Sicilian recipes and really shows the influence of the Arab and Greek cultures in our cooking.

Nana's Artichoke Frittata

1/4 C.	olive oil
8 oz.	frozen artichoke hearts
1 bunch	green onions, chopped
12	eggs
1/4 cup	milk
1 Tbs.	chopped parsley
1/2 lb.	mozzarella, shredded
dash	dried basil
1/4 tsp.	salt
1/4 tsp.	pepper

In a large 10"-12" skillet, cook onions and artichoke hearts in hot oil until golden. Beat eggs in a large bowl until frothy. Add milk and beat again. Stir in parsley, mozzarella, basil, salt and pepper. Add to onion and artichoke mixture. Mix well. Bake in oven at 325° for 15 minutes or until firm. Slice and serve warm.

Serves 6-8.

 No true Sicilian meal is complete without serving a frittata (frogia). In the sprintime, I use fresh asparagus (lightly boiled). In the winter, I may use fried potatoes, peppers and onions. I even use cauliflower and broccoli. At the restaurant, I serve this at lunch as some restaurants would an omelette. Serve this on a beautiful round platter and cut into pie slices, or as a centerpiece on your buffet.

Alexandra's Fois Gras and Pears

3 tsp.   unsalted butter
2   pears, peeled, thinly sliced
1 lb.   fois gras
pinch   salt
1/4 C.   sherry

Heat 2 tsp. butter in a skillet over medium heat. Add pears and cook about 5-6 minutes. Remove pears from pan. Set aside. Cut fois gras in half lengthwise and then across into 1/4" slices. Season with salt. Heat skillet and add 1 tsp. butter. Sear fois gras on both sides, about 1 minute. Reduce pan with sherry and cook 1 minute. Serve fois gras over pears with lightly toasted bread such as brioche.

Serves 4.

I always wonder what's going to happen when my daughter, Alexandra, goes on her first date. Will she order the fois gras as a starter? Will she request rabbit, duck or lamb the way Daddy cooks it? I feel for the boy who looks at her as if she is "pazzo." Since she was a baby, Alex would try anything Lisa and I gave her. She loves fois gras, veal, all of my pastas, and has become a true critic when dining out. But then again, did she ever have a chance?

Pepperoni Rosato Don Salvatore

17 oz. Italian tuna
6 anchovy fillets
1 C. olive oil
10 capers
4 cornichons
juice of two whole lemons
8 oz. Italian goat cheese
cracked pepper
4 roasted peppers

In a blender, add the tuna, anchovies, olive oil, capers and cornichons. Add the lemon juice and blend for 1 minute. Add goat cheese and blend until smooth. Place 1-2 tsp. of the tuna mixture on each piece of the roasted pepper. Garnish with cracked pepper.

Serves 4.

 This is another recipe I discovered in Venice during my cooking school summer at the Gritti Palace. The chef told me that Ernest Hemingway was a regular at the Palace and this was his favorite dish. We served this dish back in the late '70s, and I have added it back to my menu of late. I think it goes well with my theme, "Something old, something new."

9

Melanzane Othello

1 C.	olive oil
1	eggplant, salted and cut into 6-8 slices
8 oz.	ricotta cheese
1 Tbs.	chopped parsley
2	eggs, beaten
2 oz.	grated Parmesan cheese
4 oz.	ground Italian sausage
pinch	salt
12 oz.	tomato sauce
4 slices	Provolone

In a large skillet, heat the olive oil. Add the eggplant slices and sauté on both sides for 4-5 minutes. Take out of the skillet and place on paper towels to absorb the oil. Place ground sausage in skillet and cook through. In a large mixing bowl, blend the ricotta cheese, parsley, eggs and the Parmesan cheese. Add cooked sausage to the cheese mixture and blend together. Place 1 tablespoon of the mixture onto each eggplant slice and roll up. Place in baking dish, seam-side down, cover with tomato sauce, and bake at 400° for 10 minutes. Take out and place strips of fresh Provolone cheese on top of each eggplant roll. Broil 30-45 seconds or until cheese melts. Serve hot.

Serves 4.

The eggplant came to Sicily from the Middle East and comes in many shapes, color and sizes. I try to use the small eggplants; they are always tender. When I see Melanzana Blanco (white), I buy all I can. I am often asked the question, "Why do you leave the skin on the eggplant slices?" My reasoning is simple, it holds the tender eggplant slices together. If you want a true vegetarian dish, omit the Italian sausage.

Arancine
(Sicilian rice balls)

1 lb.	rice, uncooked
2	eggs
1/2 C.	grated cheese
	salt and pepper, to taste
1	whole onion, chopped
1-1/2 lb.	ground beef
2 Tbs.	olive oil, plus 1 C.
1/2	can tomato paste,
	mixed with a little water
2	eggs, beaten
3 C.	extra fine bread crumbs

Cook rice until tender. Drain and cool slightly. Add 2 eggs, cheese, salt and pepper. Mix well and set aside. While the rice is cooking, brown onion and ground beef in olive oil. Add the tomato paste. Let simmer for a while. Season with salt and pepper; cool. Place 2 Tbs. cooked rice in the palm of the hand. Make a well in the rice and place about 1 Tbs. of the meat mixture in the well. Mold the rice around the meat into a ball or egg shape. Dip the rice balls in beaten eggs and roll in the breadcrumbs. Sauté in hot oil until golden brown on both sides, about 3 minutes. Do not fry too close together. Remove from the oil with a slotted spoon and drain on paper towels.

Makes about 30 rice balls.

 Serve this with a little side dish of sugu. Arancine means "little oranges," and that is what they look like when cooked. This is my fvorite dish served in the "Vucciria," Palermo's outdoor market. This dish is usually reserved for holidays.

Clams Oreganato

2 doz. littleneck clams
1/2 tsp. oregano
1 oz. extra virgin olive oil
1 C. Italian bread crumbs*
lemon wedges

*ITALIAN BREAD CRUMBS
1 C. bread crumbs
1/2 C. Romano cheese, grated
4-6 garlic cloves, minced
1/2 C. fresh parsley, finely chopped

Brush outside of clams. Open the clams and rinse all sand away. Put a dab of the olive oil on each clam and cover each with a lot of the bread crumb and oregano mixture. Add 1/4 tsp. of olive oil on top of each clam and bake on cookie sheets for about 7-10 minutes at 350°, or until golden brown on top. Serve with lemon wedges.

Serves 4.

Place all ingredients except parsley in food processor. Pulse 1-2 minutes. Add parsley. Mix 30-45 seconds. Place in sealed container and store in refrigerator up to 30 days.

 A very simple but elegant appetizer. I can remember shucking hundreds of clams for parties. Arrange on a platter, 3-4 dozen, and surround with lemon slices, wedges and Italian parsley. I like to use littleneck clams. They are very tasty, not tough and cook rather quickly. They are the smallest of the hard shell family. About 1/4 cup of dry white wine added to the baking pan adds flavor to the finished product.

Carpaccio

1 lb. smoked salmon,
      or thinly sliced raw Kansas
      City strip or filet mignon

DRESSING
    2 egg yolks
1-1/2 tsp. Dijon mustard
    2 Tbs. lemon juice
    1 shallot, minced
1 Tbs. fresh tarragon, minced
1/2 C. extra virgin olive oil
    salt and pepper, to taste
    cracked pepper
    capers
    crostini slices

Place salmon or beef on chilled plate.

Whisk egg in mixing bowl. Add mustard, lemon juice, shallot and tarragon. Blend well. Add olive oil slowly, whisking, until sauce thickens.

Drizzle over carpaccio and garnish with cracked pepper and capers. Serve with crostini.

Serves 4.

This recipe is named after the 16th Century Venetian painter. I always offer cracked black pepper, a precious 12th century commodity that was controlled by the Venetians and used as currency in Europe. I served this dish at the James Beard House in 1995 to rave reviews. I have had it on the menu since then and always include it during my "receptione" or antipasti hour. Serve with Pinot Grigio or Proseco.

Focaccia Crabcakes

Crabcakes:

1 Tbs.	olive oil
1	white onion, minced
1	celery stalk, diced
1	whole green pepper, diced
1	whole pimento, diced
1 lb.	crab meat
2 C.	ground Foccaccia bread
2 tsp.	Worchestershire sauce
1-1/2 tsp.	Tabasco sauce
1 tsp.	salt
3	whole eggs

Roasted Red Pepper Sauce:

1 C.	mayonnaise
1 C.	roasted red peppers
1 C.	diced green peppers
18-20	capers
1/4 C.	minced onion
2 Tbs.	lemon juice
1/2 tsp.	Tabasco
	salt to taste

Serves 6.

For crabcakes: In a sauté pan with a little olive oil, sauté the onion, celery and green pepper. In a bowl, mix everything together but the eggs. Add the eggs, blend well and form into patties. Sauté in hot olive oil until golden and serve with the roasted red pepper sauce. *Makes 12 crabcakes.*

For the sauce: Place roasted red peppers in food processor with onions, green peppers and capers. Pulse. Add mayonnaise, lemon juice and Tabasco. Season with salt. Chill until ready to serve.

When I was asked to cook at the James Beard House in New York City, I knew I had to showcase my restaurant and offer something different and exciting. Crabcakes are always popular as an appetizer, and by adding Focaccia instead of regular bread crumbs, the texture completely changes but the flavor is outstanding and the crabcakes are very light. I serve this on a bed of chilled sauce, similar to roumelade, with roasted peppers and extra virgin olive oil; the combination really works.

Polenta con Funghi e Formagio

4 C. chicken stock
1 C. stone-ground instant
       Italian cornmeal
2 Tbs. butter
1/2 lb. Fontina cheese
1/2 C. heavy cream
    salt and pepper, to taste

Gorgonzola and Mushroom Sauce:
8 mushrooms, thinly sliced
1 pint heavy whipping cream
1/2 C. Gorgonzola cheese
1 Tbs. butter
2 oz. Marsala
1-2 sprigs fresh rosemary

Bring 4 cups of chicken stock to a boil in a 3-quart pot. Add cornmeal and cook 5-6 minutes. Whisk in butter, cheese and cream. Season with salt and pepper.

Sauté mushrooms in butter in a medium skillet. Reduce with Marsala wine. Add cream and whisk in Gorgonzola. Serve over polenta. Top with fresh rosemary.

Serves 4-6.

When my family first opened up our Trattoria on 75th Street, we were the first restaurant to offer polenta. I could not serve it the original way, a very creamy consistency, so I decided to create a sauce that would complement the polenta. The combination of Marsala and Gorgonzola works well, and I often serve this in the winter as an accompaniment to chicken, short ribs or osso bocco.

Lumache Modo Mio

1	shallot, finely chopped
1/2 C.	chopped parsley
6	cloves garlic, minced
1-1/2 C.	(12 oz. or 3 sticks) butter, softened
1-1/2 tsp.	salt
1/4 tsp.	freshly ground black pepper
6-8	assorted mushrooms, sliced thin
24	escargots, drained, rinsed and patted dry
2 oz.	white wine
4	slices garlic toast

In a bowl combine shallot, parsley, garlic, butter, salt and pepper and mix well. Chill. In a large sauté pan on medium heat, add 1 cup butter mixture.* Add mushrooms and escargots and sauté 4-5 minutes. Splash pan with wine. Serve over freshly toasted garlic bread.

Serves 4.

(*Reserved garlic butter can be used for toast or as a seasoning butter for steaks or seafood.)

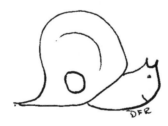

 This is one of the oldest recipes on our menu. I am surprised to see young people order this dish, but it reminds me of myself during my childhood days, always ordering something different in a nice restaurant.

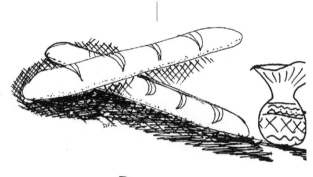

Pane

Pane

In my family bread is an essential part of our meal. Many of my recipes at the restaurant, such as panzanella, Italian bread pudding, brushetta, crostini, foccacia crabcakes and riblolita all contain my favorite breads. I am very fortunate to work with Mark Friend from Farm to Market Bakery in Kansas City. His philosophy of baking is similar to mine — simple ingredients, a biga starter, brick oven baking and a passion for what you do.

When designing menus for guests, I always try to included two or three breads. When my family gets together, it is exciting watch everyone break off the ends of the bread, never using a knife, sharing simple ingredients that brings everyone together.

Sicilian Farm Bread

1-1/2 C.	starter *(recipe follows)*
6 C.	flour
1 C.	whole wheat
2-1/4 C.	water
4-1/2 tsp.	salt

STARTER:

1 C.	flour
1 C.	water
1 tsp.	dry yeast

Mix starter and let stand 12 hours.

To make bread:
Mix all ingredients for 10 minutes. Ferment 3 hours or until dough doubles. Shape into 18 rolls or 2 medium rounds. Proof 3 hours. Mark with a knife an bake at 430° for 40 minutes until dough is browned and crisp. Let cool at least 1 hour.

My father's aunt in Sicily makes this bread for me every time I visit. I like to add 8 oz. cubed provolone before I shape the bread. I think this is one of the easiest bread recipes I have ever made. When ready to serve, place back in oven for 4-5 minutes at 350o to make crust crispy.

Casatiello (Roman Easter Bread)

SPONGE:
  4-1/2 tsp. dry active yeast
      1 tsp. sugar
  2-1/4 C. flour
  1-1/4 C. water
  1-1/4 tsp. salt

DOUGH:
        4 eggs
    4 oz. sugar
    2 oz. salt
  4-1/4 C. flour
    9 oz. butter
    2 oz. romano cheese, grated
    2 oz. parmesan cheese, grated
    2 oz. provolone, diced into 1/4" cubes
  3-1/2 oz. salami, diced
    1 tsp. pepper

Mix all ingredients of sponge for 3 minutes and let stand for 1-1/2 hours.

Mix sponge, eggs, sugar, flour, butter, romano, parmesan, pepper and salt in your mixer until smooth about 4 minutes. Add provolone and salami and let rise for 1-1/2 hours. Shape into 2 balls and place on baking tray or a mold. Let rise for another 1-1/2 hours and bake at 350° for 30 to 45 minutes.

This is a typical Easter bread shared by the Romans before the Easter meal. I like to serve it warm with extra virgin olive oil. The bread is very heavy. I also brush the top of the bread with a little egg wash for a nice crust and presentation.

Focaccia

2-1/2 tsp.   active dry yeast
2-1/2 C.   water
2 Tbs.   olive oil
7 C.   all-purpose flour (approximately)
1/4 tsp.   salt

Add all ingredients together in the mixer, Mix for about 5 to 6 minutes, until dough is smooth and elastic. Let rise for 1-1/2 hours. Place dough into a pan (oiled) and let rise for 30 minutes. Dimple the dough with your fingers, adding olive oil on top of the dough. Sprinkle salt and let rise for about 1 to 2 hours. Bake at 400° for 20 to 25 minutes. Cool and cut into small squares or triangles.

When we changed our bread selection 15 years ago at Jasper's, my father had me research a recipe for this bread. I like to top it with crushed tomatoes and fresh rosemary before baking. This bread can be used for several dishes, such as panini or in my crabcake recipe. I also like to add on top some dried rosemary, kosher salt and halved cherry tomatoes for extra taste.

Ciabatta

BIGA:
    1 C. flour
    1 C. water
  1/4 tsp. dry yeast

DOUGH:
    1 C. biga
  3-1/2 C. all-purpose flour
  1-3/4 C. water
    2 tsp. salt
    1 tsp. yeast

Mix all ingredients of biga by hand and refrigerate for 12 hours.

Preheat oven to 440°. In a mixer, add all ingredients. Mix for 18 minutes on high. Rest for 2-1/2 hours. Proof 20 minutes. Cut dough 3" into squares. Bake on baking stone 20 minutes.

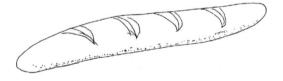

What an excellent bread and really not too hard to prepare. Ciabatta means "slippers," and that is the shape it should look like. I first had this bread in Cleveland from my friend's bakery, Orlando Brothers. In my opinion, they were the first to introduce this bread to America. This is the recipe for the bread that we serve in the dining room at Jasper's. I like to make small rolls out of this that I call chabattini.

Grissini
Roberto's Homemade Breadsticks

STARTER:
    1/2 oz.   yeast
    1/2 C.   warm water

    2-1/2 C.   room temperature water
    36 oz.   bread flour

DOUGH:
    1/2 lb.   biga (starter)
    2 lbs.   semolina flour
    1/2 oz.   yeast
    3/4 C.   olive oil
    3/4 oz.   salt
    14 oz.   wam water

Mix starter and let rest for about 10 minutes. Let the yeast work.

Mix for 5 minutes with the yeast mixture. Cover and let rise for 24 hours. This will be very wet.

Mix the yeast and the warm water and let rest for about 10 minutes. Mix everything else together and rest. Cut into 2-inch pieces. Roll to form a thin breadstick. Bake at 450° for 7-8 minutes. Let cool.

These thin breadsticks are fantastic. My friend, Roberto Donna, chef and owner of Galileo in Washington, D.C., shared this recipe with me. The biga is easy to prepare, and I use it in other bread recipes.

Insalate

Insalate

My in-between courses — some very simple but unique, others that take time and passion.

I cannot just serve a plain salad; I must dress it up, adding croutons for texture, ripe tomatoes and onions for flavor, dressings and vinaigrettes infused with spices and fruits.

When I develop recipes for a cooking class, I always spend more time with my salads, adding seasonal ingredients, thickening dressings with honey and always trying to bring them to another level.

It is very important to choose vegetables in season. The use of vegetables is based on availability and Italian tradition.

Tuscan Bean Salad

2 C.	canned white beans
1/2 C.	black Italian olives
1 C.	cubed tomatoes
1/4 C.	chopped fresh green peppers
1/2 C.	chopped celery
1/2 tsp.	red pepper flakes
1/2 C.	olive oil
1/8 C.	balsamic vinegar
	salt and vinegar to taste
1 head	radicchio

Place beans in a large mixing bowl. Add all other vegetables. Toss lightly. In a small bowl mix olive oil and vinegar with salt, black pepper and a touch of red peppers. Mix vigorously and pour over vegetables. Toss vegetables lightly again and serve in fresh radicchio cups. Chill before putting in cups.

Serves 4-6.

27

Jasper's Olives

3 lbs.	pitted or cracked green olives
3	small white onions, chopped
3/4 tsp.	salt
1/2 tsp.	black pepper
3	cloves garlic, finely minced
6 tsp.	oregano
1 C.	olive oil
3/4 C.	red wine vinegar
3	stalks celery, chopped
3	carrots, sliced
	red pepper flakes

Put all ingredients in bowl and stir occasionally. Let stand in jar or bowl for 1 or 2 days.

 This is the traditional Sicilian olive salad that has been served as Jasper's for many years. It is very popular in our market. For additional uses, place in a food processor, pulse 3-4 times, and use as a spread for sandwiches.

Asparagus with Honey Mustard

6-8 fresh asparagus spears
2-3 thin slices imported prosciutto
      ham
1 C. mayonnaise
2 Tbs. mustard
4 dashes Tabasco sauce
1 Tbs. honey
3/4 C. whipped cream
dash salt
dash pepper

In a large pot, cook the asparagus until slightly done. Take out and immediately put into ice-cold water. In a large bowl, mix the mayonnaise, mustard, Tabasco, honey, whipped cream, and the salt and pepper. Decorate the asparagus on a plate in a star shape and place a thin slice of imported prosciutto di parma over them, curled nicely. Put a teaspoon of the sauce on each side of the asparagus.

Serves 2.

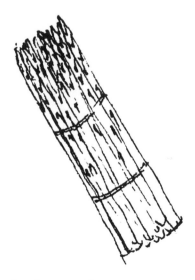

At Jasper's, we are known for the extra large asparagus we use in this dish.

29

Wild Greens and End-of-Summer Figs

1	clove garlic, crushed
8-10	figs
	balsamic vinegar
	extra-virgin olive oil
	salt to taste
3-4 C.	Italian salad greens
1 C.	mascarpone cheese
2 Tbs.	honey
1	chopped tomato
4-6	crostini (toasted crouton rounds)

In a medium-size bowl, whisk together olive oil, garlic, vinegar and salt. Slowly add honey and whisk. Add figs and let rest. Top crostini with mascarpone. Drizzle dressing on greens and serve with crostini and tomatoes.

Serves 4.

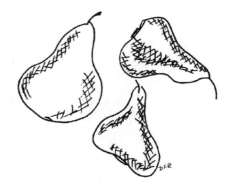

 How I remember my papa's fig tree! He would baby this tree, wrap it in the fall with straw and black tarp. By late September, the figs tasted like honey, bursting with flavor. Today, I eagerly await my first taste of figs, bringing back memories of Papa's backyard, staring at his vegetable and fruit garden, always knowing Nana was cooking something delicious from the garden.

Nana's Pomegranate Salad

2	pomegranates
1/2 C.	extra-virgin olive oil
1/4 C.	balsamic vinegar
1 Tbs.	honey
	salt and pepper to taste
4-6 C.	wild greens
1/4 lb.	gorgonzola cheese
12	crostini

Clean pomegranates and extract seeds from interior membrane. Whisk olive oil, honey and vinegar. Drizzle on greens; toss with salt and pepper. Crumble gorgonzola on top of crostini and serve alongside salad.

Pomegranates can be a bit messy. Nana always laid out newspaper, cut the pomegranates in quarters, and my brothers and myself went at those delicious morsels like candy. Whatever was left, Nana would gather and toss with a salad.

Barbabietola

4-6	red beets
8 oz.	gorgonzola
1/4 tsp.	dried oregano
3 qts.	water
1/2 C.	candied pecans
3/4 C.	extra-virgin olive oil
1/4 C.	50-year-old balsamic vinegar
4 C.	wild greens or frissee

In a large 1-gallon pot, boil beets in water until tender. Cool, peel and slice. Marinate with olive oil, vinegar and oregano and pecans. Arrange slices on greens top with crumbled gorgonzola. Serve chilled with crostini.

Serves 4.

 My brother Salvatore will not eat beets, but for some odd reason he can never get enough of these. Maybe he just loves his little brother's recipe! My good friend Steve Kokkinakis grows me fresh baby beets each summer, and I usually offer them on an antipasti table.

James Beard House Salad

1 lb.   fresh mozzarella cheese
1   zucchini
1   roma tomato, sliced
         salt to taste
1/2 C.   olive oil
4 Tbs.   balsamic vinegar
6-8   fresh basil leaves

Wash zucchini and slice into 1/4-inch slices. Dip in olive oil and place on hot grill. Cook 3-4 minutes over indirect heat. Turn and cook on other side. Place on paper towels to drain oil. Place on platters with fresh mozzarella and roma tomatoes. Drizzle with olive oil and balsamic vinegar. Garnish with basil. Add cracked pepper to taste. (For a unique salad option, try drizzling some honey on the salad.) Serve immediately.

Serves 2-3.

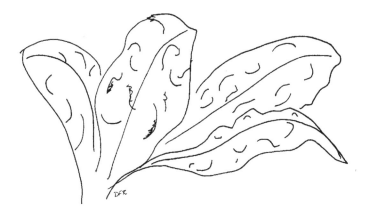

This is the salad that I served at the James Beard House in New York. When the Roma tomatoes are not ripe, just slice, dip in olive oil and grill. This gives a unique flavor. At the end of the night, leftover salad on crispy Italian bread makes for a great meal!

Panzanella "Il Lattini"

1	large loaf of Tuscan bread
2 lbs.	ripe tomatoes
1 C.	olive oil
1/4 C.	balsamic vinegar
1/2	red onion, sliced thin
10	basil leaves
16	Sicilian oil-cured olives, pitted
4	slices Italian garlic toast
	Kosher salt

In a large bowl, add olive oil and soak bread for a few minutes. Add tomatoes, onions, salt and olives. Mix with vinegar and basil and serve over crisp Italian garlic toast.

Serves 4.

This is a traditional Tuscan recipe that is really basic. I learned to make this salad in Florence while attending cooking classes, and have been serving it for over 25 years. I like to add heirloom tomatoes and fresh, crisp green beans along with boiled red potatoes. If you have fresh oregano or Italian parsley on hand, that is a nice addition. Be creative and use fresh vegetables from the garden. Remember, you must soak your bread. I prefer Kansas City's own "Farm to Market" breads.

Sicilian Orange and Olive Salad

2	whole peeled and sliced oranges
1 C.	jumbo green or black olives
	fresh basil
2 Tbs.	balsamic vinegar
1/2 Tbs.	olive oil
2 Tbs.	pine nuts
	radicchio cup
1	whole chopped red bell pepper
	pinch salt

In a large mixing bowl, add the olive oil, balsamic vinegar, salt and the fresh basil. Mix well. Add the olives and marinate overnight, or for 2-3 hours minimum. Transfer to another mixing bowl and add the orange slices, pine nuts and the bell peppers. Serve chilled inside a radiccio cup. Garnish with fresh ground pepper.

Serves 2.

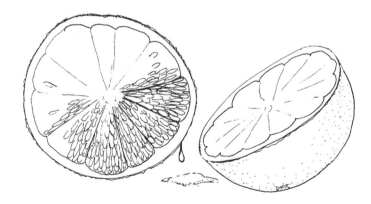

When available, I always use blood oranges, those ruby red oranges from Sicily that are as sweet as sugar and give a grand appearance to any dish.

Insalata di Spinaci e Mele

1	bunch cleaned spinach leaves
1	thinly sliced Granny Smith apple
1/4 lb.	crumbled gorgonzola cheese
1/2 C.	extra-virgin olive oil
3 Tbs.	balsamic vinegar
pinch	oregano
1 Tbs.	honey

Wash and dry spinach leaves. Mix olive oil, honey, vinegar and oregano in a large bowl. Mix with gorgonzola and sliced apple. Toss with spinach leaves and add cracked pepper and salt. Serve chilled.

Serves 4.

 This salad is still on our menu today, and depending on the season, we may add fresh berries, oranges or pineapple. Fresh, crispy croutons always give a nice crunch with the apples.

Insalata di Calamari

2-1/2 lbs. squid
juice of 1/2 lemon
1/2 C. fruity olive oil
4 Tbs. balsamic vinegar
3 cloves garlic, lightly crushed
coarse salt and freshly ground
pepper to taste
1 Tbs. minced fresh basil leaves
2 tsp. minced fresh mint leaves

To clean the squid, carefully pull the head and tentacles from the body sac. Cut the tentacles above the eyes. Pop out the little ball or beak in the center of the tentacles. Discard it and the innards. Pull out the quill-shaped bone in the body sac and discard. Peel off the skin. Thoroughly rinse the interior of the body and the tentacles. Drain. Cook the body and tentacles in boiling salted water in two separate saucepans with lemon juice for 20 minutes, or until tender. Drain well. Cut the body into rings. Leave the tentacles whole or, if large, cut in half. Combine the squid in large bowl with the olive oil, vinegar, garlic, salt and pepper. Cover and marinate overnight in the refrigerator. Sprinkle with the herbs. Toss gently, seasoning with salt and pepper. Adjust the dressing, adding more oil and vinegar if necessary.

A refreshing, fragrant salad with tender squid, fresh basil and mint that give this salad a marvelous summery feeling. Buy the smallest squid available and cook it until it loses all traces of rubberiness. Squid is exceedingly tender when properly cooked. To keep the flesh pure white, cook the body of the squid separately from the tentacles, since the skin of the tentacles releases color into the cooking water which will turn the flesh a pale pink. This salad can be made several hours in advance.

37

Insalata Fantasia con Mascarpone Crostini

6 C.	mixed field greens
1	clove garlic, minced
3/4 C.	extra-virgin olive oil
3 Tbs.	balsamic vinegar
pinch	salt
pinch	tarragon
6-8	strawberries, thinly sliced
1 Tbs.	honey
4-6	mascarpone crostini

Mix olive oil, vinegar and garlic. Whisk in honey and herbs. Toss with field greens and berries. Top with fresh mascarpone crostini.

Serves 4-6.

 A little secret here— this is the recipe for my Tuscan salad dressing now sold in many stores in the Midwest.

Sicilian Green Bean Salad

1 lb.   fresh green beans
2   red potatoes
1/2   red onion
1/2 C.   olive oil
        fresh basil
3 Tbs.   red wine vinegar
        salt and pepper to taste

Wash potatoes. Clean and cut green beans. In a large pot of water, boil potatoes until done. Add the green beans and boil approximately 15 to 20 minutes longer. Drain and set aside to cool. Slice the onion and add to the potatoes and green beans. Add seasoning, oil and vinegar. Toss well.

Serves 6.

Oh, so simple, but yet so Italian and traditional. In the summer, toss with chopped tomatoes, olives and serve over warm Italian toast.

Classic Caesar Salad

1	clove garlic
3	anchovy fillets
1/2	lemon
1/2 tsp.	Lea & Perrins worcestershire sauce
2 tsp.	wine vinegar
1/2 cruet	olive oil
1	egg
1 head	Romaine lettuce
1 Tbs.	Parmesan cheese
1 C.	croutons
10 grinds	cracked black pepper

In a large wooden bowl, add a little salt to the bottom. Add the garlic and mash up with a fork and add the anchovies and make it all into a paste. Add the juice of the lemon and mash it up more. Add the vinegar, oil and the Lea & Perrins. In a separate bowl, add Romaine. Add egg and toss. Add the dressing and toss. Add the cheese and croutons and toss. Serve chilled with cold forks. Offer fresh ground pepper on top.

Serves 2.

 This is Jasper's traditional recipe, still used at the restaurant for our most popular salad. My father insisted on serving this salad on a chilled plate with ice-cold forks. This is our most requested recipe and my family's favorite.

Pasta

Pasta

No Italian cookbook can be complete without recipes for pasta, either slow simmering sauces or quick five or six ingredient dishes. Pasta is the soul of the Italian table, bringing families together for centuries.

When choosing my pasta, I look at what sauce I am using, something short or a special cut, something handmade or from a high quality bronze dye cut. Sometimes the simple sauces, dressed up with just extra virgin olive oil and a few vegetables, are more satisfying. Here I offer a variety.

Italians have been producing, sharing and eating pasta for centuries, and it is with the same pride I share my favorite dishes.

A word of note to the wise cook: for 20 years I always tested the doneness of pasta by throwing it against the wall to see if it would stick. Today's kitchens are a little different, and I know my wife Lisa does not appreciate this technique, even though I have convinced my daughter Alex this is the only true test in the Mirabile kitchen.

Classic Marinara

1	28-oz. can San Marzano tomatoes
4	cloves minced garlic
1/4	whole minced onion
6-8	leaves fresh basil
1/4 tsp.	red pepper
	pinch salt
1/4 C.	olive oil

For sauce: Sauté the onion in olive oil until translucent. Add garlic and salt and continue to sauté for an additional 1-2 minutes. Add the crushed tomatoes and seasonings. Cook for 25 minutes.

This is a base sauce for many of my recipes. I also like to serve this over pasta, plain and simple. As an added favorite, use fresh asparagus, mushrooms, peas or eggplant.

Sicilian Pasta con Sarde

1 lb.	cauliflower
1/2 C.	pine nuts
1/2 C.	raisins
10-12	basil leaves, or 1 tsp. dried basil
1	fennel bulb, boiled and diced
1	onion, diced small
10-12	sardines (canned)
2 Tbs.	grated pecorino cheese
4 oz.	extra virgin olive oil
1 lb.	Italian pasta, buccatini or thick macaroni
1/2 tsp.	salt
	red pepper flakes
1/2 C.	toasted bread crumbs
2	28-oz. cans tomato puree

Soak the raisins in warm water for 30 minutes and drain. Clean the cauliflower; remove the outer green leaves and the core from the stalk end. Break the cauliflower into pieces, then break off florets. They must be very small in order to cook in a few minutes. Boil salted water to cook the pasta and the cauliflower. Add cauliflower, cook for 5-8 minutes until tender. Peel and chop the onion and sauté it in a frying pan with the olive oil. Add garlic and cook for 1 minute on medium heat. Add sardines, raisins and fennel to garlic mix. Toast pine nuts for 3 minutes on high until lightly browned. Sauté a few minutes. Add tomato puree and season with basil, red pepper and salt. Simmer, stirring occasionally. Add pasta to water and cook until al dente. Drain pasta and cauliflower, toss into a large bowl. Add sauce, more fresh basil and grated pecorino cheese. Sprinkle with toasted bread crumbs. Serve hot.

Serves 8-10.

 This is the most popular and well-known Sicilian pasta dish. You can buy the Pasta con Sarde in a can and add it to your favorite tomato sauce recipe. The toasted bread crumbs are a must; they represent St. Joseph and the wood shavings because he was a carpenter. This tradition has been passed down for centuries.

Reno's Sicilian Pasta

1 C. extra virgin olive oil
3 cloves garlic, crushed
3 sprigs fresh mint, crushed
4 spears fresh asparagus
1/4 tsp. crushed red pepper
12 peeled shrimp
1/2 C. Sicilian bread crumbs
1/4 C. Italian parsley, chopped
1/2 lb. rigatoni

Bring 2 quarts water to boil. Add pasta and stir. Cook until al dente. In a large sauce pan, heat olive oil. Add shrimp and asparagus and sauté until cooked 4-5 minutes. Add garlic and take off stove. Add red pepper, parsley and mint. Drain pasta, reserving some of the water. Toss pasta with olive oil mixture, add Sicilian bread crumbs and continue to toss. Use reserved water, chicken broth or olive oil if pasta is too dry. Serve hot.

Serves 2-3.

 The bread crumbs represent St. Joseph, the patron saint of Sicilians. My cousin Reno in Sicily makes this dish without shrimp, but I think the addition gives the sauce and pasta some needed texture and flavor. I like to add anchovies with the garlic for added flavor. A lot of chefs in Sicily add shaved botagga, a hard brick of dried tuna roe.

Cappellini Melanzane Alla la Scudera

2 whole large eggplants, sliced
1 C. olive oil
4 C. Mama's tomato sauce*
1 lb. angel hair pasta, cooked
1/2 C. fresh mozzarella cheese
4 tsp. grated Parmigiano Reggiano
10-12 fresh basil leaves

Mama's tomato sauce recipe can be found on page 68.

To assemble:
Slice eggplant 1/4 inch thick, and lightly salt each slice. In a large skillet, heat olive oil and sauté eggplant 6-8 minutes on each side. Place on paper towels and pat excess oil off.

In a sauté pan toss angel hair with pomodoro sauce and fill each eggplant with pastas. Sprinkle with both cheeses and top with more marinara sauce. Bake at 450° for 15-20 minutes. Serve at once.

Serves 4-6.

This was one of the first pastas I discovered during my travels to Sicily. La Scudera translates to the Stabies and is a famous restaurant in Palermo, Sicily. You can prepare this dish ahead of time and warm just before serving. I sometimes use a becamel sauce instead of the tomato sauce.

Jasper Jr.'s Pasta Dough

2 lbs. flour
8-10 eggs
1 Tbs. oil
salt

Place flour in a large mound on a wooden chopping block. Add salt and oil and make a well in the middle of the flour. Add eggs and begin to mix by hand. Mix thoroughly 3-4 minutes. Knead 1 minute. Wrap in cellophane and refrigerate until ready to use.

 My basic pasta dough recipe is used for Jasper's lobster ravioli, pumpkin ravioli and our homemade tortellini.

Pasta Con Melone E Prosciutto

1 lb. fettuccine
1 medium size cantaloupe
(overripe)
1 C. Reggiano Parmigiano cheese
1-1/2 C. heavy cream
4 oz. butter
1/2 C. diced prosciutto di parma
salt and pepper to taste

Cook pasta according to package directions. Set aside. Peel 1 cantaloupe and seed. Cut into 1/2-inch pieces. In a large sauté pan add butter and heat. Add cantaloupe and prosciutto, sauté with salt and pepper until melon is soft, about 3-5 minutes. Add heavy cream and bring to a boil. Add pasta and toss until pasta is evenly coated. Add cheese and continue tossing. Serve hot. Do not make ahead.

Serves 4.

This is a popular pasta during the summer months. I use only cantaloupe; no other melon will work. The combination of prosciutto and melon is a natural.

Leonardo's Pasta Primavera

1/2	diced onion
1 C.	diced fresh tomato
1 C.	broccoli
1 C.	cauliflower
1 C.	zucchini
1/2 C.	peas
2 tsp.	minced garlic
1 1/2 lb.	butter
4 oz.	olive oil
4 C.	chicken stock
	salt to taste
	pepper to taste
1/2 tsp.	oregano
1/2 C.	white wine

In a large stockpot, bring 4 quarters of water to a boil. Add pasta of your choice and cook al dente. In a large sauté pan, sauté cauliflower in half the butter and the olive oil. Add the rest of the vegetables with the garlic and oregano, wine, and season with salt. Simmer until vegetables are al dente. Add chicken stock, olive oil and butter. Simmer about 10 more minutes. Serve over your favorite pasta.

Serves 3-4.

 This is my brother Leonard's recipe and one of my family's favorites. It is great in the spring. Be creative with this recipe — use green beans, colored peppers, mushrooms or other fresh vegetables. Serve over penne or linguine.

Uncooked Tomato Sauce

1/2 C.	extra virgin olive oil
1-1/2 tsp.	salt
1-1/2 tsp.	red pepper flakes
20	pieces basil, chopped in half
2	28-oz. cans tomatoes
18 cloves	minced garlic

In a large skillet, heat olive oil and sauté garlic 3-4 minutes. In a large bowl, add tomatoes, salt, basil and red pepper. Mix by hand, crushing tomatoes. Add olive oil and garlic. Let sit 2-3 hours.

This is our popular summer sauce — a raw, uncooked tomato sauce that is great on pasta, grilled fish or chops. You may want to add fresh mint for flavor or even some lemon when marinating chops.

Farfalle al Porcini

6 oz.	dried porcini mushrooms
16 oz.	boiling water or chicken broth
1/4 lb.	butter
16 oz.	cream
2 Tbs.	mustard
1 Tbs.	parsley
1 tsp.	salt
1/4 tsp.	red pepper flakes
2 oz.	brandy
1 lb.	farfalle (bowtie pasta)

Add porcini mushrooms to boiling water or chicken broth; let steep 20-30 minutes. Strain. In a medium saucepan, melt butter; sauté mushrooms 2-3 minutes. Reduce pan with brandy add cream, red pepper, salt, mustard and parsley. Sauce will thicken in 2-3 minutes.

Cook pasta according to package directions. Strain, add sauce, toss and sprinkle with grated Romano cheese.

Serves 4.

 We serve this sauce over polenta or tortoloni. I served this sauce at the James Beard House over sea bass. As an added touch, I also add asparagus, fresh mint and gorgonzola cheese for more flavor.

Cannelloni Cappricio

FILLING:

4 oz.	finely chopped prosciutto
16 oz.	fresh ricotta
4 oz.	ground cooked Sicilian fennel sausage
2 Tbs.	Reggiano Parmigiano
2	eggs
1/4 C.	chopped parsley

PASTA:

2 C.	flour
2	extra large eggs
2 Tbs.	olive oil
	pinch of salt
1 C.	béchamel sauce
	(Recipe on page 54)

FILLING:

Place all ingredients in mixing bowl and stir until all ingredients are mixed evenly.

PASTA:

Place flour in a mound on a pastry board. Make a well in the middle and add the eggs and oil with the salt. Mix the dough and knead 5-10 minutes. Place dough in a pasta machine and stretch to 1/16 of an inch. Cut into 6x6 squares.

To assemble: Lay out dough pieces and add 2 Tbs. of filling to each square. Fold over and crease at top. Brush with egg wash.

To bake: Place 1 cup béchamel sauce on the bottom of a baking dish and add cannelloni. Top with more sauce and bake 15-20 minutes. Serve piping hot.

This recipe has been on our menu for over 40 years. Add a touch of tomato sauce to the béchamel, and you will have my "pink sauce."

Pappardella Con Anitra "Modo Mio"

ROASTING DUCK:

1	cleaned duck
1 C.	celery
1	peeled onion
1 C.	diced carrot
	salt and pepper to taste
1	orange

Preheat oven to 400°. Place duck breast side up in large roasting pan. Fill cavity with carrots, onions, celery and orange. Roast for 1-1/2 hours. Let cool. De-bone and shred duck.

SAUCE:

2	(28 oz.) canned San Marzano tomatoes
3/4 C.	diced onion
8	cloves minced garlic
1/2 C.	olive oil
1-1/2 tsp.	salt
1/2 tsp.	red pepper flakes
1 C.	chianti
	fresh basil
1 tsp.	fennel
1 lb.	pappardella

In a large pot, sauté onion in olive oil until onion caramelizes. Add garlic and take off stove. Add tomatoes, chianti, red pepper flakes, fennel and salt. Place back on stove and cook 1 hour. Add roasted duck and simmer. Add basil. Cook pasta according to package directions. Serve sauce on top of pasta, and dust with grated romano.
Serves 6.

Modo mio translates to "my way," and this is my personal favorite. The red pepper really adds great flavor. I serve this dish in the fall and winter, or serve it over freshly made polenta.

Béchamel Sauce

3 C.   milk
1 Tbs.   finely chopped onion
1/8 tsp. nutmeg
4 Tbs.   unsalted butter
         (preferably clarified)
6 Tbs.   flour

Combine the milk, onion, nutmeg and pepper in a small saucepan; bring to boil over moderate heat. Immediately remove the pan from the heat, cover tightly and set aside for 10 minutes. In a heavy 2-qt. saucepan, melt butter over low heat. Remove pan from the heat; stir in flour with a wire whisk to make a smooth roux. Return to a low heat and, stirring constantly, cook for 2 minutes or until roux foams. Pour into milk mixture and beat vigorously with whisk until the roux and liquid are blended. Scrape the sides of the bowl to make sure all of the roux is incorporated into the sauce. Increase the heat to moderate and, still stirring constantly, cook until the béchamel sauce comes to a boil and thickens enough to coat the wires of the whisk heavily. Reduce heat. Simmer the sauce and take off heat. Strain the sauce through a fine sieve — set over a bowl, pressing down gently.

This is really my basic white sauce. I sometimes add a bit of sweet sherry wine. We serve this dish over canneloni and various chicken dishes.

Shrimp and Artichoke Risotto

5 Tbs.	unsalted butter
2	cloves garlic
1 lb.	medium shrimp shelled and deveined
12	artichoke hearts, sliced lengthwise
2 Tbs.	minced fresh parsley
5 C.	fish stock or 2-1/2 cups bottled clam juiced diluted with 2-1/2 cups water
1	large white and tender leek, thinly sliced
1-1/2 C.	Arborio rice
1/2 C.	dry white wine
1/4 tsp.	freshly ground pepper
	salt

In a large skillet, melt 2 Tbs. of the butter. Add the garlic and cook over low heat until softened, about 2 minutes. Increase the heat to moderate, add the shrimp and cook, stirring occasionally, until just opaque, 1 to 2 minutes. Add parsley and set aside.

In a medium saucepan, bring the broth to a simmer. Maintain at a simmer over moderately low heat.

In a large non-corrodible 3-qt. saucepan, melt the remaining 3 Tbs. of butter over moderate heat. Add the leek and cook until softened, 3 to 4 minutes. Add artichoke hearts. Reduce pan with wine. Add the rice and stir for 1 to 2 minutes until well-coated with the butter and slightly transparent. Add the wine and cook until it evaporates. Continue to add broth until rice cooks. Add all seafood and artichokes. Serve immediately.

Serves 4 to 6.

I like to add some Parmigiano Reggiano at the end for more flavor. I also make this with squid ink and top it off with 24K gold. This is unique and edible and also great for presentation.

Cavatelli al Lumache

4 tsp. butter
1/4 tsp. olive oil
12 escargots (snails)
1/4 C. fresh green peas
1/4 C. diced San Marzano tomatoes
6 oz. heavy cream
4 Tbs. freshly grated Parmigiano
 Reggiano
16 oz. cooked cavatelli
 salt
 pepper

Melt butter and olive oil in a frying pan with escargots. Sauté it for 2 minutes and add tomatoes, salt and pepper and cook one more minute. Add heavy cream and cook 1 more minute. Add cooked pasta and toss with cheese and peas. Sprinkle with freshly chopped parsley.

Serves 2-3.

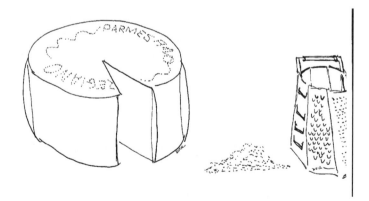

This was a popular dish when our restaurant was on 75th Street. The pink sauce is created by mixing tomatoes and cream. This is great as a side dish when serving steaks or chops.

Rigatoni alla Caruso

3 Tbs. julienne onions
5-6 large sliced mushrooms
8-10 large chicken livers
1 oz. cream sherry
8 oz. tomato sauce
2 oz. olive oil
12 oz. rigatoni

Sauté onions until golden; add the mushrooms. Cook for about 4 minutes until tender. Add the chicken livers and cook until done. Add tomato sauce and the wine. Simmer for about 3 minutes, pour over cooked rigatoni.

Serves 2-3

 I just put this dish back on my menu and received a great response from customers. This is really a traditional dish from Naples.

Fettuccine Pope John XXIII

1/4 lb.	green fettuccine
1/4 lb.	egg fettuccine
1/2 C.	butter
1 C.	prosciutto ham
1	egg yolk
1/2 C.	peas
2 C.	cream
4 Tbs.	grated Parmigiano Reggiano

In a large pot of boiling water, cook the pasta until al dente. In a large skillet, melt the butter and add the prosciutto ham. Sauté for 3-5 minutes. Add the cream and bring to a boil. Take off heat. Add the noodles, peas, egg yolk and the cheese. Toss well. Sprinkle with fresh ground black pepper.

Serves 2.

 My father discovered this dish in the early '60s while in Rome. He was dining at a restaurant near the Vatican, and the owner made him a dish that he created for the Pope. When my father came home, he recreated the dish and started serving it to his friends.

Pasta Fagiole

2 C.   whole chopped carrots
1 C.   whole chopped onions
1 C.   chopped celery stalks
1/4 lb.   chopped pancetta
        (Italian bacon)
2   whole potatoes, peeled and cut
        into 1/4-inch
3   whole chilies, chopped fine
        in food processor
2 lbs.   packaged cannellini beans
4 tsp.   salt
1/2 tsp.   red peppers
1-1/2 tsp.   crushed black pepper
2 C.   canned tomatoes
        (put in processor)
2 C.   dried ditalli pasta

Put beans in pot and cover with water. Water should be about 3 inches above beans. Add tomatoes and cook about 1 hour until beans are just cooked. In a frying pan, sauté pancetta until lightly crisp. In another pan put all vegetables except potatoes in a little oil and fry until just halfway tender. Add all to pot with the beans and tomatoes and cook about 15 minutes. Adjust seasoning to taste. Add 1 cup dry ditalli pasta and potatoes and cook for another 15 minutes. Serve hot.

Serves 8-10.

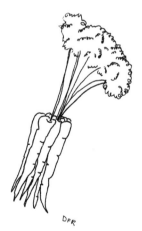

 I love to add some type of greens to this dish, whether it is escarole or baby spinach. I also drizzle some extra virgin olive oil on top of the soup before I serve. This is one of my most requested winter recipes. I suggest you serve this over bread.

Fettuccine Con Panna E Formaggio

1/2 lb.   fettucine noodles
4 Tbs.   butter
2 C.   heavy cream
1 C.   grated Parmigiano Reggiano
         cheese
       salt and pepper

Cook pasta in 2-1/2 to 3 qts. of boiling water al dente (when the pasta is done but has a bit of firmness to it). Drain. Heat the butter and cream in a pan large enough to hold the pasta. Add the pasta to the pan and heat. Add cheese and heat. Toss gently, being careful not to break pasta. Add salt and pepper to taste.

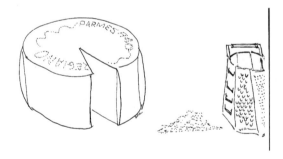

This dish was always to be prepared tableside at Jasper's and was very popular in the '70s. Today, our customers request broccoli, mushrooms and grilled chicken added to the traditional recipe from Alfredo's of Rome.

Bucatini alla Amatriciana

6 Tbs.	chopped prosciutto ham
6	slices chopped bacon
1/2 C.	chopped onion
2 tsp.	minced garlic
	pinch of red pepper
	pinch of salt
28 oz.	marinara sauce*
1 lb.	bucatini
1/4 C.	grated Pecorino Romano

Recipe on page 43

Sauté the prosciutto, bacon and onion together until onion is translucent and bacon is crispy. Add the garlic and red pepper and cook for 3 minutes. Add the salt and the marinara sauce and cook 4-5 minutes. Cook pasta according to package directions. Spoon sauce over pasta and add grated Pecorino Romano.

Serves 2-3.

 Although this dish is usually credited to the Romans, it was created in the Marches and Umbria, from the town of Amatrice. The Amatrice also serve it over the fatter bucatini with a hole in the middle.

Jasper's Pasticcio Di Melanzane E Ricotta

6 C. prepared béchamel sauce*
1 C. olive oil
2 medium eggplant,
     sliced 1/4-inch thick
1 C. Parmigiano Reggiano
15 slices mozzarella
3 lbs. ricotta
1/2 tsp. salt
1/2 tsp. pepper
4 Tbs. butter
5 whole eggs
1/4 C. parsley

Prepare the bechamel sauce. Set aside. Mix the ricotta, eggs and parsley together and set aside. In a large skillet, add the olive oil. Heat, add eggplant and cook on both sides. Lightly salt. Place on paper towels and pat dry. Preheat the oven to 350°. Cook lasagna noodles. Drain. Coat bottom of a 10x14x3 baking dish with butter. Layer with the bechamel sauce. Sprinkle with parmisian cheese. Layer 6 sheets of lasagna. Layer ricotta mixture, mozzarella and eggplant. Repeat 3 times. Layer top with ricotta and bechamel sauce. Sprinkle with Parmigiano cheese. Bake for 45 minutes and let set for 10 minutes before cutting. Serve hot.

Serves 8-10.

*Béchamel sauce recipe on page 54.

This is a unique lasagna that I serve during the winter months. It is also good with cooked spinach layered in between the eggplant.

Jasper Jr.'s Slow Pasta

1 C. extra virgin olive oil
3 cloves garlic
3 sprigs fresh mint, crushed
4 spears fresh asparagus
1/4 tsp. crushed red pepper flakes
12 snails (canned, drained and rinsed)
1/2 C. Sicilian bread crumbs
1/2 lb. flat, cut pasta squares

Bring 2 qts. water to a boil. Add pasta and stir. Cook until ad dente. In a large sauté pan, heat olive oil. Add snails and asparagus and sauté until cooked, 4-5 minutes. Add garlic and take off stove. Add red pepper, parsley and mint. Drain pasta, reserving some of the water. Toss pasta with olive oil mixture, add Sicilian bread crumbs and continue to toss. Use reserved water and more olive oil if pasta is too dry. Serve hot.

Serves 2-3.

 This is a unique pasta dish I created for Slow Food USA and for my press luncheon at Jasper's to introduce Slow Food to Kansas City. I use snails because that is the "mascot" of Slow Food. I like a flat pasta for this dish in which you can make fresh pasta and cut little squares.

Spaghetti alla Puttanesca

1 lb.	cooked spaghetti
1 C.	olive oil
6	anchovies
1/2 C.	black olives
2 Tbs.	capers
4 C.	prepared tomato sauce
1 Tbs.	chopped parsley
1/4 tsp.	crushed red pepper flakes
	salt and pepper to taste

Dice anchovies and olives. Sauté in olive oil for about 4 minutes. Add capers. Add sauce and simmer. Add cooked pasta and mix well over a low flame and sprinkle with fresh Italian parsley and crushed red peppers and serve hot.

Serves 4.

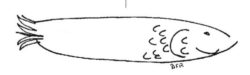

 The puttanesca sauce is great with poached halibut or lemon sole. A nice addition to this sauce are some sautéed shrimp and scallops

Linguine alla Pesto

2-1/2 C. pureed fresh basil
    3 cloves chopped garlic
   1 C. heavy whipping cream
  1/2 C. grated parmesan cheese
  2/3 C. olive oil
  1/2 C. pine nuts
  1 tsp. salt

In a pesto place the fresh garlic and pine nuts with the salt, and use a mortar to chop really fine. Add the fresh basil and continue to chop. Place all ingredients with heavy cream, olive oil and cheese and puts in food processor and blend until sauce is fine. Place sauce in sauté pan and heat.

Cook 1 lb. pasta in rapidly boiling water and cook al dente. Drain and add to pesto sauce and toss until pasta is well-coated. Served hot.

Serves 10.

 This pesto sauce is excellent when served chilled over various cuts of pasta. An egg noodle pasta is also suggested with this sauce. The true Genovese sauce has diced potatoes and green beans in it.

Penne alla Vodka Con Pomodoro Secci

1 lb.   penna (tubular pasta)
5 Tbs.   unsalted butter
2/3 C.   Polish or Russian vodka
1/4 tsp.   red pepper flakes
1   16 oz. can Italian plum
       tomatoes, drained, seeded
       and pureed
3/4 C.   whipping cream
1/2 tsp.   salt
3/4 C.   grated Parmigiano cheese
4 oz.   sun-dried tomatoes
       cut into 1/4-inch strips

In a large pot of boiling, salted water, cook the penne until al dente (tender but still firm) 8-10 minutes.

Meanwhile, melt the butter in a large, non-corrodible skillet, over moderate heat. Add sun-dried tomatoes and sauté 3-5 minutes. Add the vodka and the hot pepper flakes, and simmer for 2 minutes. Add the pureed tomatoes and the cream; simmer for 5 minutes longer. Season with the salt.

When the pasta is al dente, drain well and add to the skillet with the hot sauce. Reduce the heat to low. Add the cheese and mix thoroughly. Place into a heated bowl and serve at once.

Serves 6.

When I was younger, I would make this dish on TV. I always attracted some attention with the vodka by flaming it as I poured it into the pan.

Linguini San Remo

2 oz.	olive oil
6-8	shrimp
6-8	scallops
3 oz.	cleaned crab legs
3 oz.	cleaned lobster meat
1 tsp.	minced garlic
10 oz.	marinara sauce*
4 oz.	whipping cream
pinch	red pepper
	flour for dusting
1/2 lb.	linguine

Dredge the seafood in flour and sauté in olive oil for 3 minutes. Add the garlic and cook another minute. Add the marinara sauce and the cream and cook 2-3 minutes. Add salt and pepper to taste and the red pepper. Serve over freshly cooked linguini.

Serves 2-3.

Recipe on page 43

 Still on the menu today. I like to add calamari and mussels to this.

Mama's Tomato Sauce (Sugo)

28 oz.	tomato puree
4 C.	water
1	whole head pureed garlic
2	chopped onions
1 tsp.	salt
1/2 tsp.	red pepper
2 Tbs.	sugar
2 Tbs.	fennel seed
1/2 tsp.	sweet basil

In a 4-qt. pot sauté minced onion in olive oil until translucent. Add garlic and take off stove. Add tomato puree and water. Mix thoroughly. Add seasonings. Cook approximately 2 hours. After 1-1/2 hours add sugar and basil. At this time you can add sautéed sausage, meatballs and brasole.

Serves 8.

This is the old-fashioned sauce used by Jasper's and Marco Polo's. If you do not like canned puree, you can substitute whole tomatoes. Omit the water. You need to puree these tomatoes on the food processor or by hand. Make sure you consistently stir the sauce and do not let the sugar burn or you will scorch the sauce.

Linguine alla Vongole

1 lb. linguine
2 lbs. littleneck clams
4 oz. olive oil
4 cloves garlic
1 Tbs. parsley
pinch red pepper flakes
8 oz. clam juice
2 oz. white wine
pinch oregano

Steam clams in a large pot until they open. Place in frying pan with olive oil and garlic. Sauté 1-2 minutes. Reduce pan with wine and clam juice. Add seasoning and serve over linguine.

Serves 4.

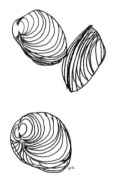

 My family has been making this classic dish for over 75 years. Never put cream or cheese in this dish. In Italy it would be a sin.

Piatti del Giorno

Piatti del Giorno

My special dishes of the day, recipes that I have treasured over the years. I have chosen some of the most popular veal, poultry, seafood, beef and lamb dishes. Most of the recipes, except for a few, can be prepared quickly and without much prep work.

Every Italian family has their favorite dishes, and here you will find our favorites. Many have been passed down for over a century.

To work in our restaurant, a cook must not only learn my piatti del giorno, they must learn to pick up flavor, season properly and do this consistently. Over the years, I have trained some excellent cooks, and I am always impressed when they remind me of an ingredient I may have forgotten.

Some of my dishes are determined by seasonal availability and tradition, but always with respect, love and generous hospitality.

Mom and Dad's Italian Meatloaf

4 lbs.	hamburger
2 lbs.	veal
2 lbs.	pork
3 C.	bread crumbs
8	eggs
2	small green peppers, chopped
2	carrots, chopped
1	can sweet peas
3/4 C.	red wine
1-1/2	chopped onion
2 Tbs.	sugar
1 tsp.	red pepper
1 tsp.	oregano
2 Tbs.	taragon
2 tsp.	sweet basil
1 tsp.	cumin
2	pieces garlic, chopped
2 tsp.	salt
1 tsp.	black pepper
1/2 tsp.	nutmeg

GLAZE:
1/4 C.	honey
1/4 C.	brown sugar

Mix all ingredients in large bowl. Place in baking loaf pan and cook at 350° for 1/2 hr. Take out of oven and put mixture of 1/4 C. honey and 1/2 C. brown sugar in a paste and spread with a knife over partially cooked meatloaf. Return to oven and cook 45 minutes longer or until meatloaf is cooked. Let cool, then warm when ready to eat.

You may be asking, why a meafloaf recipe? This is one of my parents' favorite dishes, and my dad was very proud when his recipe was requested by a local newspaper.

Pollo alla Frederico

6	chicken wings
5	chicken breasts
3	legs
4	thighs
12	pieces Italian sausage
5	red green peppers, julienned
2	onions (julienne)
1	can peas and juice
5	potatoes (cubed 1" size)
1	28 oz. can tomatoes, blended
16 oz.	white wine
4 C.	water
	salt to taste
2 tsp.	red pepper
1 tsp.	sweet basil
3/4 tsp.	tarragon
1/4 tsp.	rosemary
3/4 tsp.	thyme

Sauté chicken and sausage 1/2 way. Sauté onions and peppers 1/2 way. Put all in roaster pan, add wine, tomatoes, peas with juice, plus seasonings. Stir well. Bake in oven 450° 30 minutes. Add potatoes and mushrooms. Stir well until potatoes are cooked. Add peas. Stir. Add more salt or pepper as desired.

Serves 8-10.

Many of my friends and family know this recipe as "Chicken Fred." My father spent many hours perfecting this recipe, and I am sure he would be proud that I shared it with everyone.

Roasted Pork Loin

3-3-1/2 lb.	boneless pork roast
3	fennel bulbs, chopped
1	onion, chopped
fresh	rosemary
	salt and pepper to taste
1 C.	Marsala wine
12	thin slices prosciutto ham
6	thin slices mozzarella
3 oz.	Parmigiano Reggiano
3 C.	cooked escarole
1/2 C.	Italian bread crumbs
4 oz.	butter
	pan drippings

Pound out pork with meat pounder until thin in between 2 pieces of clear wrap or waxed paper. Sprinkle with the bread crumbs, layer with escarole, prosciutto ham and parmigiano and mozzarella cheese. Carefully roll up the pork like a jelly roll and wrap with a string. Bake in a 350° oven for 25-30 minutes with chopped fennel and onions. Slice thin and serve with Marsala wine sauce made with pan drippings and butter. Serve with the roasted fennel and onions from the roasting pan.

 I always serve this dish during the Easter season and when available. I substitute capretto (baby goat) or lamb. The flavor is outstanding!

Nana Jo's Grilled Lamb Chops

4-5	sprigs fresh mint
1/2 C.	olive oil
2-3	cloves garlic, thinly sliced
1/2 C.	mint jelly
1	lime
	salt to taste
5 Tbs.	balsamic vinegar
2-3	racks lamb
	brown sugar

Cut racks into chops. Drizzle with lime juice. Mix olive oil, brown sugar, salt and balsamic vinegar. Let marinate overnight with mint. Fire up the grill. Place chops on grill and cook to desired temperature. Make a sauce with mint, olive oil, mint jelly and garlic. Brush chops while on the grill with mint sprig brush. Use this sauce for dipping chops. Serve hot off the grill.

Every summer, my Nana would prepare these delicious little chops on the grill. She would marinate the chops in balsamic and garlic and a little bit of red pepper. My three brothers and I would eat the chops faster than my dad could grill them! This is a favorite at Laura O'Rourke's Culinary Center of Kansas City, where I frequently do cooking classes.

Pollo Alla Valdostana

1 lb. boneless, skinless chicken
 breast
2 whole beaten eggs
2 tsp. Italian breadcrumbs
20 raisins
20 baby capers
4 slices extra-thin prosciutto ham
4 slices Bel Paese cheese
8 oz. strong chicken stock
1 Tbs. butter
4 oz. olive oil
1/4 C. lemon juice
1/4 C. sherry

Cut chicken breast into eight 2 oz. portions and pound them until they are about 4 inches long and about 3 inches wide.

Brush each piece with fresh beaten egg and place the prosciutto ham and Bel Paese cheese on top of four of the chicken pieces; then top those four pieces with the capers and raisins and sprinkle with a little dusting of the Italian breadcrumbs. Place remaining chicken breast portions on top of each of the topped chicken pieces and press down lightly (so that it looks like a sandwich).

Place the chicken in the refrigerator to chill and firm for about half an hour.

Remove chicken from refrigerator, dredge in flour lightly, and then into the beaten egg. Heat olive oil and butter in a skillet and gently add the chicken Valdostana and sauté for approximately two minutes on each side, until golden. Sprinkle with sherry and lemon juice.

Remove the Valdostana from the pan and deglaze it using the chicken stock and salt and pepper to taste. Spread the sauce on a plate and arrange the Valdostana on top. Garnish with a sprig of sweet basil.

I served this dish to Frances Mayes, author of Under the Tuscan Sun, *my favorite all-time book. She thought the recipe was as authentic as she has ever had in Italy.*

Jasper's Scampi alla Piedmontese

1 lb.	shrimp, cleaned and deveined
1 Tbs.	butter
1 tsp.	extra virgin olive oil
1	shallot, chopped fine
1	garlic, chopped
1/8 tsp.	black truffle peeling
1/2 tsp.	heavy cream
1 C.	Pinot Grigio
1/4 C.	salt and red pepper to taste

Sauté shrimp in butter and olive oil. Cook 3-4 minutes. Add garlic and shallots. Cook 1 minute. Reduce pan with Pinot Grigio. Season with salt and red pepper flakes. Add heavy cream and truffle shavings. Bring to a light boil and serve.

Serves 4.

The first time I ate this dish was in the region of Piedmonte. It was covered with black truffle shavings. Truffles are very expensive, but give off an aroma not found in any other ingredient.

Roasted Cornish Hen
Balsamic and Dried Fig Reduction

2 lb.	Amish poussin or cornish hen
1/2	onion
1/2	blood orange
1/2 Tbs.	rosemary, dried
1/2 C.	balsamic vinegar
1/4 C.	brown sugar
6-8	sun-dried figs, quartered
1/8 tsp.	salt
1/4 C.	butter

Set oven to 400°. In a large roasting pan, pour 1/2 of balsamic vinegar in the bottom. Clean cornish hen, fill with quartered orange and onion. Rub with salt and butter, glaze with brown sugar, and place in roasting pan. Sprinkle with rosemary and lightly pour balsamic vinegar on chickens. Add dried figs, roast in oven 45 minutes until golden. Use glaze to drizzle.

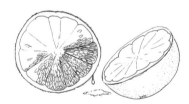

This is one of my new dishes that is becoming a popular item on the menu. You can substitute dried cherries or cranberries for the figs.

79

Oxtails Braised in Barolo

3-4 lbs.	oxtails
1	bottle (750 ml.) Barolo wine
2	stalks celery, coarsely chopped
2	medium onions, chopped
28 oz.	San Marzano tomatoes
2	sprigs rosemary
2 tsp.	salt
8-10	baby carrots, chopped
1/2 tsp.	red chile peppers
1/4 C.	butter
2 oz.	brandy
4	potatoes, cubed 3/4"

In a large skillet, heat butter and sear oxtails. Flash pan with brandy. Season with salt. In a large roasting pan, add onions, carrots and celery. Add oxtails and wine, crush tomatoes by hand, add chiles and rosemary.

Roast in 375° oven for 3 hours. Add potatoes and cook remaining 45 minutes. Serve at once.

This is a great dish to serve over homemade pasta such as pappardella. Oxtails tend to be a little greasy, but remember, that is where all the flavor is.

Pollo Toscanini

4 oz.   Italian sausage
4 oz.   skinned boneless chicken
       breast
1 Tbs.   chopped black olives
1/4 C.   sliced mushrooms
1/8 C.   peas
1/2 C.   Italian tomato sauce
       pinch oregano
2 oz.   balsamic vinegar
3 oz.   butter
1/2 tsp.   chopped fresh parsley
       salt and pepper to taste
2 oz.   olive oil

In a large saucepan, sauté chicken and sausage pieces in the 2 oz. of butter and 2 oz. of the olive oil for 3 to 5 minutes. Add the mushrooms and cook for 1 minute longer. Add the tomato sauce and balsamic. Sauté with the black olives. Simmer for 3 to 5 minutes. Add the peas and the seasonings. Serve immediately.

Serves 4.

 This dish is excellent served over fresh pasta noodles. I like to serve this in the winter with fresh risotto and an array of winter squashes. This dish is not on the menu any longer, but still requested and prepared weekly.

Pollo Con Porcini

4-6 oz.   chicken breast
4 Tbs.   butter
4 oz.   dried porcini
1/8 Tbs.   pepper
1/8 Tbs.   salt
1/4 C.   whipping cream
         fresh thyme and Parmigiano
           Reggiano to taste

To reconstitute the porcini mushrooms, place them in a small pot of boiling water. Let stand for 30 minutes. In a large skillet, add the butter and porcini mushrooms. Sauté for 3-4 minutes or until porcini are tender. Add the juice of the porcini and cream and cook down for about 5 minutes or until sauce thickens. In another sauté pan, cook chicken breasts 4-5 minutes on each side. Add sauce. Sprinkle with fresh parmigiano and thyme. Serve immediately.

Porcini mushrooms are a specialty Italian mushroom and can be found in Italian markets or through a mail order catalog. I like to use veal instead of chicken, and I serve this on a bed of bow tie pasta.

Vitello alla Florentine

4 oz. olive oil
    4 8-oz. veal leg slices,
        pounded thin
      flour
3 oz. white wine
    2 lemons
2 Tbs. butter
      pinch of tarragon
      salt and pepper to taste
      thin slices of fontina cheese
      creamed spinach
      (see following recipe)

In a large skillet, heat olive oil over medium heat. Dust veal with flour and sauté 2-3 minutes on each side. Reduce pan with wine and lemon juice. Add butter and seasonings. Top each veal slice with spinach and Fontina. Place lid on pan for 3 minutes until cheese melts. Serve on platter and drizzle sauce on top.

I prefer a veal chop pounded thin for this dish. You can use a pork chop and follow the same procedure.

Creamed Spinach

6 C.	cups fresh spinach
3	slices chopped Pancetta (Italian bacon)
1 C.	finely chopped onion
1	clove finely chopped garlic
1 T.	flour
1/2 tsp.	salt
1/2 tsp.	pepper
1-1/2 C.	milk

Cook spinach and drain well. Sauté bacon, onions and garlic together for 10 minutes or until onions are tender. Remove from heat. Add flour and seasonings. Mix well. Return to heat. Add the milk gradually, and stir until thick. Add spinach and mix well.

This dish is especially good served on top of veal or chicken. I like to eat this as a side dish. P.S. My daughter, Alexandra, rates all other creamed spinach recipes against her daddy's.

Pollo Alla Marsala Con Funghi e Fontina

1 lb.   chicken breast, pounded thin
3-4 oz.   wild mushrooms, sliced thin
2-3 oz.   Marsala wine
    flour for dusting
2 Tbs.   butter
2 Tbs.   olive oil
    8   slices of fontina cheese
    salt to taste

Dust the chicken in the flour. Heat the butter and oil in a large skillet. Sauté the chicken on both sides about 2 minutes. Sauté the chicken on both sides about 2 minutes. Sauté the mushrooms when you turn the chicken over for the second side. Reduce with Marsala wine and add salt and continue to reduce. Layer the chicken with the fontina slices and cover the pan until the cheese melts. Serve on a platter.

Marsala wine was discovered by an Englishman in the 1700s. This Sicilian wine is widely used throughout Italy from appetizers to desserts. I use a sweet marsala for this dish.

Edit

Delete

Pollo Alla Chiantiagna

1 lb.   chicken breast
2 Tbs.   butter
2 C.   chianti
1/4 C.   Tuscan olive oil
16   sliced mushrooms
1/4 lb.   prosciutto ham, diced
2 C.   marinara sauce
2   cloves garlic, minced

Melt butter in large skillet. Cut chicken into small pieces, dust with flour, add to sauté pan and cook 2-3 minutes on each side. In a separate pan, sauté garlic in olive oil, add mushrooms and prosciutto ham and sauté. Add chianti and reduce. Add marinara sauce and chicken. Serve over polenta.

Serves 4.

 This is one of my Tuscan dishes that I had many years ago outside Cortona. It is originally served with wild rabbit or quail. I have been using chicken and veal, and my customers really like it.

Braised Short Ribs Sangiovese

5 lbs.	short ribs
1	bottle (750 ml.) Sangiovese wine
2	stalks coarsely chopped celery
2	medium chopped onions
28 oz.	San Marzano tomatoes
2	sprigs rosemary
2 tsp.	salt
8-10	chopped baby carrots
1/2 tsp.	red chile peppers
1/4 C.	butter
2 oz.	brandy
4	potatoes, cut into 3/4-inch cubes

In a large skillet, heat butter and sear short ribs. Flash pan with brandy. Season with salt. In a large roasting pan, add onions, carrots and celery. Add short ribs and wine, crush tomatoes by hand, add chiles and rosemary. Roast in 375° oven for 3 hours. Add potatoes and carrots and cook remaining 45 minutes. Serve at once.

Serves 2-3.

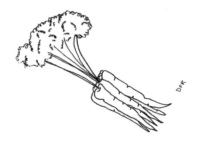

This is a great dish to serve over homemade pasta such as pappardella.

Grilled Sea Bass

4	8-oz. cuts fresh sea bass
4 oz.	Pinot Grigio wine
4 oz.	butter
1 C.	heavy cream
2 tsp.	truffle shavings
	salt to taste
1 tsp.	dry tarragon

Grill sea bass filets. In a 1-qt. pot, bring wine and butter to a boil. Whisk in cream. Add truffle shavings and tarragon. Serve over sea bass with lobster potatoes.

I serve this dish on my new menu at Jasper's. The lobster potatoes can be addictive. You can substitute salmon or swordfish and experiment with various herbs and wine.

Pesce San Giuseppe

4	5 oz. filets of sole
2 C.	fine Italian bread crumbs
1 C.	flour
2	eggs, beaten
1/4 C.	milk
1/2 C.	cooking oil

(*Jasper's chilled seafood sauce on page 90.)

Cut sole into serving size portions. Place bread crumbs in a bowl. Combine eggs and milk. Dip the sole in the egg mixture; drain and coat well with the Italian bread crumbs. Heat 2 to 3 Tbs. oil in a 12" skillet. Arrange fillets in a single layer in the skillet. Fry over moderate heat for 5 to 8 minutes or until browned on both sides and sole can be flaked easily with a fork, turning fillets only once. Repeat process and fry remaining fish. Drain on paper towels. Serve with fresh lemon and seafood sauce.*

Serves 4.

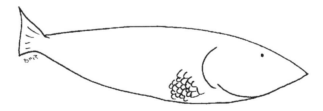

 This is a traditional dish served in many Sicilian homes. For a crispier dish you can skip the bread crumbs and use grated romano cheese only. I like to make my own version of tartar sauce and serve with this dish.

Jasper's Chilled Seafood Sauce

1	white onion
3	stalks celery
1	whole green pepper
1	whole red pepper or pimiento
2 C.	mayonnaise
1/2 tsp.	red pepper
1 tsp.	salt
	juice of 1/2 lemon

Put onion, celery, green and red pepper into a Cuisinart and blend. Fold in mayonnaise, add the red pepper, salt, lemon and mix together. Serve chilled.

This sauce is always served at my home with chilled shrimp or crab. At Jasper's, I sauté fresh sole with a Parmigiano crust and also serve this sauce alongside the dish.

Quaglia Grigliata Alla Mirtilli Rossi

4 semi-boneless baby quail
1 C. cooked wild rice
1/2 chopped tomato
1/4 chopped onion
4 oz. Sicilian fennel sausage

SAUCE:
1/4 C. butter
16 cranberries
1/4 C. sweet marsala
1/4 C. orange juice
1 sprig fennel

For the stuffing: In a small skillet sauté onion until golden. Add the tomato and sauté. Add sausage and brown. Add wild rice and a tablespoon of butter. Stuff quail with filling.

Place quail on a large rack and brush with butter. Bake at 400° for 12-15 minutes.

Sauce: In a large skillet poach orange juice with cranberries. Cook until cranberries crack. Add butter, fennel and marsala and reduce. Place sauce on platter and place quail on top. Garnish with cranberries and fresh fennel. Serve hot.

Serves 4.

This dish is good with a lot of pepper. If you use salted butter, be careful with the salt in the last step.

Vitello alla Valdostana

1 lb.	veal slices, 2 oz., pounded thin
2	whole beaten eggs
2 tsp.	Italian bread crumbs
20	raisins
20	baby capers
4	slices extra thin prosciutto ham
4	slices Bel Paese cheese
1 C.	strong veal stock
1 Tbs.	butter
4 oz.	olive oil
1/4 C.	lemon juice
1/4 C.	cream sherry

Start with a whole veal tenderloin and cut it into 2-oz. portions. Pound two of them thin until they are about six inches long and four inches wide. Brush each piece with fresh beaten egg and place the prosciutto ham and bel paese cheese on top of one slice. Add the capers and the raisins and sprinkle with a little dusting of the Italian bread crumbs. Place the other piece of veal on top and press down lightly so it looks like a sandwich. Put it in the refrigerator to shape and rest for at least half an hour. Take it out of the refrigeration and dredge in flour lightly and then into the beaten egg. Heat a skillet with the oil and butter and dip the Valdostana in the frying pan and cook about 2 minutes until golden. Flip it over with a spatula and sauté on the other side for 2 minutes and sprinkle with the sherry and the lemon juice. Take the Valdostana out of the pan and deglaze the pan with the veal stock and salt and pepper to taste. Arrange the plate with the sauce on the bottom and the Valdostana on top.

You can easily substitute chicken breast for the veal slices.

Scampi Fra Diavlo

3 oz.	olive oil
16	jumbo shrimp, cleaned and deveined
1/2 C.	mushrooms, sliced fresh
1/2 tsp.	garlic, crushed fresh
2 oz.	white wine
24 oz.	Jasper's marinara sauce *(Recipe on page 43)*
1 lb.	pasta pinch, cooked al dente red pepper flakes

In a large sauté pan, heat the olive oil. Dust the shrimp lightly with flour and sauté on each side for 2 or 3 minutes. Add the mushrooms and sauté for another minute. Add the garlic and cook for a minute and add 2 oz. white wine. Add the Jasper's marinara sauce and the red pepper flakes. Serve the sauce over the fresh-cooked pasta. Serve immediately very hot. Add extra red peppers if desired.

Serves 4.

This is a spicy dish. Fra Diavlo is "from the devil," hot and fiery.

Sicilian Involtini

2   8 oz. boneless chicken breasts,
        pounded thin
2   prosciutto hams, sliced thin
2   balls of fresh mozzarella cheese,
        sliced thin
    capers and raisins
4 Tbs.   olive oil

FOR THE SAUCE:
1/4 C.   white wine
         juice of 1/2 lemon
2 Tbs.   butter
         pinch salt
1/4 C.   strong chicken broth
         fresh oregano

Cut the chicken breasts in half and pound the chicken thin. Pat dry. Put a piece of the fresh prosciutto ham on the chicken breast and a layer of the mozzarella. Sprinkle on the raisins and the capers. Roll the chicken and secure with toothpick. Dip in egg wash and Italian bread crumbs. Sauté in olive oil and turn when golden. Take the chicken out of the pan, remove toothpick, and place on a hot plate. In the same sauté pan, add the white wine, butter, lemon, salt and chicken broth and cook down.

Serves 2.

The first time I ate this dish was in Palermo, Sicily. My father and I worked on this recipe when we came home, and it is still on our menu today.

Vitello alla Limonata Dore

8	slices veal (scallopini), about 1-1/2 lbs.
	salt and freshly ground pepper to taste
1/2 lb.	eggplant, peeled and cut into 8 1/4-inch-thick rounds
	flour for dredging
2	eggs, lightly beaten
1 C.	fine fresh bread crumbs
1 C.	butter
8	thin, seeded lemon slices
1 tsp.	oregano
1 Tbs.	chopped parsley
3 Tbs.	olive oil
3 Tbs.	lemon juice
1/8 tsp.	oregano
2 oz.	sherry wine

Pound the meat lightly with a flat mallet and sprinkle with salt and pepper.

Sprinkle the eggplant rounds with salt and pepper. Dredge in flour and shake off the excess. Dip in egg, then in bread crumbs. Pat to help the crumbs adhere. Heat the half cup of oil and cook the eggplant pieces on both sides until golden. Drain on paper towels.

Dip the pieces of veal in flour and shake off excess. Dip in egg to coat each piece well. Heat the 3 tablespoons of oil and the butter in a skillet and cook the veal, 2 or 3 pieces at a time, until golden. Turn and cook on the other side. Continue until all the meat is cooked. Splash with lemon and sherry.

Arrange the veal on a platter, slices slightly overlapping. Top each slice with an eggplant round and lemon slice. Sprinkle with oregano and parsley and serve hot.

The original Veal Limonata in Kansas City. This is the same recipe that appeared in Craig Clairbone's Veal Cookery, and my father was proud to share it with the author.

Marco Polo's Italian Sausage, Fried Potatoes, Peppers and Onions

2	green or red bell peppers
1	white onion
2	Idaho potatoes
4 Tbs.	olive oil
	salt
1 lb.	link sweet Italian sausage
4	hoagie rolls, centers removed

Cut the onion crosswise into 1/2-inch-thick slices. Cut peppers in half and remove seeds, cut the same way. Peel and slice potatoes 1/4-inch think. Place olive oil in skillet on medium heat, add potatoes and cook for 10 to 12 minutes, turning once. Add peppers and onions and cook 8-10 minutes. Take off heat and set aside.

On a grill, over low heat, grill Italian sausages for 20 minutes or until they are no longer pink in the center.

Serve sausages on stop of a bed of warmed potatoes, peppers and onions or place sausages into a hoagie roll and top with potatoes, peppers and onions.

Serves 2-3.

*The dish that put Marco Polo's on the map. I started grilling sausages on 75th Street in 1984, and this is **the** most popular dish at our market today.*

Flaming Peppered K.C. Steak

4	14-oz. Kansas City sirloin steaks
	salt to taste
1-2 Tbs.	crushed black pepper
2 oz.	butter
1/2 oz.	minced shallots
	brandy, splash
8 oz.	heavy cream
2 Tbs.	orange marmalade
6 oz.	worchestershire sauce

Season steaks generously with black pepper. Place on hot grill and cook to desired temp.

In a large sauté pan, add butter and place on heat. Remove steaks from grill. Add shallots to sauté pan and cook 1-2 minutes on high heat. Carefully flame pan with brandy. Add marmalade. Cook another minute. Add cream and worchestershire sauce. Let simmer until sauce starts to thicken. Add more salt and pepper to taste. Serve immediately.

Serves 4.

My father flamed this dish tableside at Jasper's for 40 years. All of my brothers would learn this, Caesar salad and fettucini Alfredo, and work the dining room preparing this dish.

Dolce
E
Bevande

Dolce E Bevande

If you look up the word "dolce" in an Italian dictionary, you will see the word "sweet," plain and simple. Italians love their sweets, whether it be granita in Sicily, gelato in Rome or a crostata in Florence.

At Jasper's, all meals must end with a sweet from our dessert cart. Ricotta cheesecake, tiramisu, strawberry chantilly, creme brulee — the list goes on and on. My favorite is fresh strawberries with balsamic drizzled on top. But how can I pass up our cannoli, a recipe handed down for centuries in the Mirabile family?

I have also included some recipes for homemade Italian cordials which I love to serve on a warm winter evening by the fireplace, or on a hot summer day in a chilled glass. Our lifestyle is often referred to as "la dolce vita," the sweet life, and my recipes follow that saying.

Cannoli

1 lb.   ricotta
1 C.   confectioner's sugar
2 drops   cinnamon oil
1/4 C.   chocolate, diced
1/4 C.   candied orange and cherries,
          diced
6   cannoli shells

In a large mixing bowl, add ricotta. Fold in powdered sugar. Add candied fruit, chocolate and cinnamon oil. Chill 2-3 horus in refrigerator. Fill shells with cannoli cream; dust with confectioner's sugar.

Serves 6.

This is definitely the most traditional and popular of all Sicilian desserts. I recommend straining the ricotta for an hour to take out most of the water.

Our Flaming Bananas

4 Tbs.	butter
4 Tbs.	brown sugar
2	ripe bananas, quartered
dash	cinnamon
1-1/2 oz.	banana liqueur
1-1/2 oz.	dark rum
4 dips	vanilla bean ice cream

Melt the butter in a chafing dish. Add the brown sugar and blend. Add the banana and sauté. Sprinkle with the cinnamon. Pour in banana liqueur and the rum, ignite, basting bananas with the flaming liquid. Put one dip of ice cream in glass. Service bananas on top when flame dies out.

Serves 3-4.

When I have special events at the Culinary Center of Kansas City, I like to serve this dish. My wife Lisa does not like cooked fruit but does eat this dessert when I prepare it.

My Tiramisu

2-1/2 lbs. mascarpone
6 egg yolks
1 C. sugar
1/2 C. powdered sugar
1 Tbs. almond extract
2 oz. amaretto
2 oz. brandy
cocoa powder
36 ladyfingers
3 C. espresso coffee

Separate eggs. In a mixing bowl whip sugar and coddled egg yolks until blended. Add mascarpone cheese, almond extract, amaretto and brandy until fluffy. Wrap a 10-inch cake pan with Saran wrap on the inside and put about 1/3 of the cheese mixture on the bottom. Soak ladyfingers in espresso coffee one by one and make a layer on the bottom of the cheesecake pan. Put 1/3 of the cheese mixture on top and smooth it out and sprinkle a little cocoa powder on it. Put another three layers the same way and let it set in the refrigerator overnight.

Loosen from ring and invert so the bottom is now the top. Decorate with espresso coffee beans.

Serves 12.

 This classical Venetian dessert can be made with sponge cake instead of ladyfingers and made in a large bowl, lining sides with ladyfingers or cake. Mascarpone is Italian cream cheese that is found in Italian specialty markets.

103

Pesche al Vino Chianti

10-12 whole peeled and sliced fresh
        peaches
  1 750 ml. bottle Chianti
 1 C. sugar
 1 qt. fresh white chocolate ice cream

Skin the peaces and cut into 8 pieces. Sprinkle with sugar and let sit for 1 hour. Add Barolo wine and let sit for another 2 to 3 hours. Dip about 4 oz. of wine and a few pieces of the fresh peaches over a dip of the fresh homemade white chocolate ice cream.

Serves 8.

 I can never remember a holiday without this dessert. My father would spend hours adjusting the recipe, adding mint, cinnamon sticks, cloves, etc. Sometimes we would serve it warm in the winter; in the summer, always chilled. This was one of the desserts served at my wedding.

Crostata di Ricotta

TART CRUST:
- 1 C. butter
- 1/2 C. sugar
- pinch salt
- 2 eggs
- 3 C. flour

Cream butter and sugar. Add eggs. Stir in flour and salt. Roll dough 1/8 inch thick. Fit dough into greased tart pans. Line with foil and fill with beans or pie weights. Bake in preheated 400° oven for 12-15 minutes.

FILLING:
- 15 oz. ricotta
- 1 C. sugar
- 4 eggs
- 3 tsp. flour
- 2 Tbs. freshly squeezed orange juice

Combine all filling ingredients and mix well. Turn into tart crust. Bake 25 minutes at 350°. Place on wire rack and cool. Decorate with berries and whipped cream.

Serves 6-8.

 This is truly a classic Sicilian tart. I like to add candied fruit and chopped chocolate to the ricotta mix. A nice blood orange sauce is also good and makes a great plate presentation.

Crema di Pani "Mio Modo" (Bread Pudding)

1/4 C.   melted butter
1 lb.   Italian bread cut up in cubes
3 C.   milk
1 C.   cream
3   whole beaten eggs
1-1/2 C.   sugar
1 tsp.   nutmeg
2 Tbs.   almond extract
1 C.   chopped figs (dried)
1 C.   sliced almonds

SAUCE:
1 C.   powdered sugar
1   whole beaten egg
1 C.   melted butter
1 C.   amaretto

Mix cream and eggs together and stir in other ingredients. Place in well-greased loaf pan. Bake at 350° for 45 minutes.

SAUCE:
Prepare a double boiler. In a small pot, add butter and sugar. Cook 2-3 minutes. Add egg and cook over low heat until slightly thick. Whisk in amaretto. Serve hot over sliced bread pudding.

This is my recipe for bread pudding that my grandmother would make for me. She made a lemon sauce that was to die for, but I came up with the amaretto. You can substitute dried apples for the figs.

Pepe Raguna's Cantucci

6	eggs
1 lb.	sugar
2 lbs.	flour
	grated lemon
2 Tbs.	hazelnuts, chopped
1-1/2 Tbs.	baking powder
1 tsp.	vanilla

Mix all ingredients. Roll into fist-size balls and then roll each ball into 8" long strip. Bake at 350°. Remove from over and cut into 1/2" pieces. Return to oven and bake 10 minutes. Cool 1 hour. Serve with Vin Santo.

Pepe Raguna lives in Sicily, and when we visit his home, he always has these savory treats in his living room after dinner.

Cielege Al Vino Chianti con Semi Freddo

2 qts.	Bing cherries (canned)
1	750 ml. bottle Chianti
2	cinnamon sticks
1 C.	sugar
1/2 gal.	fresh vanilla bean gelato

In a 4-qt. pot, add bing cherries, cinnamon sticks, sugar and wine and bring to a soft boil. Steep 20 minutes. Dip about 4 oz. of wine and cherries over a scoop of the fresh homemade gelato.

Serves 10.

 Now this sauce can be addictive! You may want to add 1/4 cup of cornstarch and mix with cold water. Add to the boiling cherries for a thicker sauce. Substitute pound cake for the gelato, or use both for a really rich dessert.

Jasper's Dessert Crepes

8-10 crepes
1 C. chilled pastry custard*
1/2 C. sugar
1 oz. Grand Marnier
1 oz. triple sec
3/4 C. butter

CREPE MIXTURE:
1-1/2 C. flour
2 Tbs. sugar
pinch of salt
3 whole eggs
1-1/2 C. milk
1/2 tsp. orange flower water

(*recipe on page 112)

Fill each crepe with 2 tsp. pudding. In a large skillet, add 1/2 cup butter. Heat and add the filled crepes. Sauté and add the sugar. Flame with the Grand Marnier and the triple sec. Add the rest of the butter and make a sauce. Serve immediately.

TO MAKE CREPES:
Sift the flour, salt and sugar in a large bowl. Add the eggs, milk and the orange flower water. Whisk for 2-3 minutes and place in the refrigerator. Let set for 2 hours.

Although this recipe is French influenced, my father always had this dish on our dessert menu. You can add fresh berries and different liqueur when flaming.

Zabaglione

3 egg yolks
3 Tbs. sugar
3 oz. sweet Marsala wine
seasonal berries

Warm the egg yolks and the sugar in a double boiler over a low heat, and then whip them with a wire whisk. Pour marsala into the egg yolks, drop by drop, and keep beating. The mixture will begin to foam and then swell into a light, soft cream. Do not overcook or it will collapse. Serve over fresh berries.

Serves 2.

 Cinnamon and grated lemon rind may be added before pouring in the marsala, and this liqueur in turn can be replaced with a high-quality white, sweet, dry or sparkling wine. Brandy or cherry brandy may also be added.

Vuccere Sfinge

1 C.	boiling water
	cash of salt
1 large Tbs.	Crisco
1 C.	flour
3	eggs
	honey

Bring water to boil. When water is boiling, remove from heat and add the flour, dash of salt and the Crisco. Beat well with a fork. Add the eggs, one at a time. Spoon into hot oil deep fryer and cook about 5 minutes with rack over at 350°. Strain. Sprinkle with powdered sugar and drizzle honey on top.

Serves 6.

 My Nana and mom would always make these for me. These are the famous "doughnuts" of the Sicilian outdoor market, "The Vuccere," in Palermo. Street vendors sell these by the dozen in little brown paper sacks. Be careful — they are addictive!

Pastry Custard

5	egg yolks
2/3 C.	sugar
1/3 C.	flour
1/2 tsp.	vanilla powder
2 C.	hot milk
1 Tbs.	butter

Beat egg yolks thoroughly. Combine sugar and flour and salt and beat into egg yolks. Add mixture to the hot milk and cook over hot water until thick.

Makes 2 cups.

Nana Josephine, as my mom is called today, makes this wonderful custard for our restaurant. We fill cream puffs, napoleons, our cakes and even layer with fresh berries and toasted coconut. Grazie Nanni!

Cremé Brulee

1 qt. heavy whipping cream
6 egg yolks
1/2 C. sugar
3 C. sugar
1 vanilla bean
7 Tbs. softened butter
1/2 C. brown sugar

In a large metal bowl set over a bain marie, whisk the egg yolks and sugar together until the mixture is thick. Add vanilla bean. Remove from heat. Carefully whisk in the cream. Pour custard in individual cups and bake at 375° for 45 minutes. Chill until serving time. Add sugar on top and place under a broiler until golden. A blow torch will accomplish the same task. Chill until serving time. Top with berries and fresh mint sprig.

Serves 12.

I started making this dish when we moved to our 103rd Street location. I like to use a blow torch to caramelize the sugar; it really is a great effect.

Jasper Jr.'s Affogato

4 scoops vanilla gelato
  4 shots fresh brewed espresso coffee

Place ice cream scoops into 4 cappuccino cups. Pour a shot of espresso on top. Serve immediately.

*Invite guests to pour the espresso over the ice cream and eat with a spoon while it melts. Dust cup with cocoa and a fresh mint sprig. Serve with biscotti.

 Il Caffe was the name of my family's coffee shop when we were located in Waldo. This was one of my specialties. I love to serve this to my friends, it is so simple to make, very refreshing, light and undoubtedly Italian.

Panettone Ripieno di Gelato

4	beaten egg yolks
1/2 C.	sugar
1/2 rind	grated orange
2 C.	cream
1/4 C.	Grand Marnier
1	beaten stiff egg white
1 lb.	panettone

(Panettone is a typical Lombard sweet bread, which in the old days was made in the shape of a dome. Today it is more like a wide, inflated tower.)

Beat the egg yolk, sugar and orange rind in the top of a double boiler until thick and lemon-colored. Stir in the cream. Place over gently simmering water and cook until the mixture is thickened , stirring frequently.

Remove from heat and add the Grand Marnier. Beat the egg white until stiff an fold into the custard. Transfer to an ice cream maker and churn until frozen. (If you are not using the ice cream right away, store in the freezer until shortly before serving time.)

Cut a cap from the top of the panettone and scoop out most of the inside. Fill with the ice cream. Put the cap back on and place in freezer for 24 hrs. To serve, cut in wedges and drizzle with chocolate or caramel sauce. *Serves 6.*

 This is a traditional Italian holiday bread that I have filled with gelato. You can use store-bought gelato, your favorite flavor, and follow the same procedure for filling. My recipe was featured in Cucina magazine.

Tartuffo Tre Scallini

2 C.	white chocolate ice cream
8	maraschino cherries/hazelnuts
1-1/2 C.	chocolate shavings
1/2 C.	freshly whipped cream
8-10 Tbs.	chocolate syrup
1 C.	fresh seasonal berries

With a large ice cream scoop, make baseball size balls of the white chocolate ice cream. Shove a cherry into the center of each ball. Freeze for 30 minutes. Roll in chocolate shavings and keep frozen. When ready to serve, pour chocolate syrup over tartuffo. Place on chilled plate and decorate with freshly whipped cream and more chocolate shavings. Place a fresh mint sprig in the middle of the tartuffo and dress with fresh berries. Serve immediately.

Serves 4.

The famous frozen ice cream ball looks like a big truffle. My father would always take me to Tre Scallini in Rome to enjoy this dessert. I still go to the Piazza Navona in Rome, have this dessert, and reminisce.

Cannoli Ice Cream

2 drops oil of cinnamon
2 drops clove
4 oz. candied fruit
1/4 C. chopped chocolate chips
2 C. sugar
2 qts. cream
8 egg yolks
1/2 tsp. vanilla

Combine all ingredients, except the chocolate chips and candied fruit, into a saucepan and cook over medium heat until the consistency of custard.

Cool mixture and pour into ice cream machine and freeze according to manufacturer's directions (approximately 45 minutes). Fold in chocolate chips and candied fruits, then freeze.

Makes 1/2 gallon.

This is a classical Sicilian gelato that my cousin still serves in his coffee shop today. It tastes just like a cannoli and should be served in the summer. This recipe won 1st Place in the American Dairy Council's search for a new ice cream flavor in 1995.

Tuscan Vin Brule (Hot Mulled Wine)

1	750 ml. Chianti
1/2 C.	sugar
2	cinnamon sticks
8	cloves

Place all ingredients in a large pot. Bring it to a slow boil and take it off the stove. Put a lid on it and let it steep for 15 to 20 minutes. Serve warm in espresso or cappuccino cups

Serves 6.

I was served this drink during the winter in Tuscany at Badia Coltibouno by Lorenzo DéMedici. It is great with some fresh fruit and biscotti.

Nana's Amaretto

1 C. water
1 C. granulated sugar
1/2 C. brown sugar
2 C. vodka
2 tsp. vanilla extract
2 Tbs. almond extract

Combine the sugars and melt with the water. Bring to a boil and immediately take off the fire. Let cool. Add the extracts and vodka. Place into a covered and sealed Mason jar and let sit at least 2 weeks. Serve by the ounce after a great Italian dinner.

Makes 24 oz. of amaretto liqueur.

 You may see me serving this in the dining room out of a Mason jar. It looks like bootleg whiskey, and my customers get a kick out of seeing this.

Cousin Reno's Granita

8   lemons — halved
1 lb.   sugar
1-1/2 liter   water

Squeeze the lemons into a bucket. Put half the lemon rinds into a separate container with the water. Let them soak for about 5 minutes. Strain the lemon juice into the water and add sugar. Place in a 1-gallon pot and bring to a boil. Take off heat and cool for 30 minutes. Serve with biscotti and a sprig of fresh mint.

My family has been making granita and gelato in Gibellina, Sicily, for over a century. Today, my cousin Jasper (Reno) still serves this dish from May–September. People line up for this treat after dinner, but true Sicilians eat this for breakfast in between a small roll. When I visit, my cousin makes blood orange granita, from the delicious blood oranges grown in Sicily.

Anisette

750 ml vodka
1 C. water
2 C. sugar
1 oz. anisette flavor

Make simple syrup of the sugar and water. Add alcohol and flavoring. Add 3 Tbs. clear Karo syrup.

 When I was younger, my father would sit at the kitchen table and make this special Anisette. Our cousins from New Jersey gave him the recipe, and we still serve it today.

Papa's Homemade Hazelnut Liquor

1 C.	water
1-1/2 C.	sugar
1/2 C.	brown sugar
4 tsp.	vanilla extract
2 C.	vodka
3 Tbs.	hazelnut extract

Combine sugars and melt with water. Bring to a boil. Let cool. Add extracts and vodka. Place in a covered and sealed Mason jar and let sit at least 2 weeks.

This looks like bootleg whiskey from the 1920s when stored in Mason jars. Add to coffee or heavy cream as an after-dinner drink.

Limoncello alla Sorento

STEP 1:
    12   lemons
1 liter   grain alcohol

Cut lemons in half, remove seeds only. Add alcohol. Let sit 12 hours.

STEP 2:
1.5 liter   water
700 grams   sugar

Boil sugar and water to make syrup. Add to alcohol mix. Let stand approximately 4 weeks.

Strain and bottle. One time I let it stand about 8 weeks, and the limoncello was a bit clearer, but tasted the same. Store the finished limoncello in the freezer. Don't worry, it won't freeze! Serve as a liquor or drizzle over fresh gelato.

 I also like to make Crema Limoncello, same process. When finished after 4 weeks, I strain and add 2 cups Eagle Brand Condensed Milk to mixture and shake, place in bottles and refrigerate only. DO NOT FREEZE!

Per Finire
April 2003

As I sit on a ferry ride from Reggio Calabria, Italy to Messina, Sicily, many thoughts are going through my mind — how my grandparents traveled this same route, the Messina straits, and wonder where my family would be today if Nana and Papa did not immigrate to America, how my father influenced me and inspired me to write my cookbook.

My thoughts and memories continue. I close my eyes and imagine myself living in Sicily today. It is such a beautiful country. For centuries, this exotic, mysterious island was the crossroads of commerce. Every culture came together in Sicily, leaving as a tribute the richest bounty of food and spices imaginable. I am dreaming of the Vucceria, Palermo's outside market, strolling down the street, stopping by the produce stalls, eating blood oranges and figs. I can taste the capretto as my thoughts wander. I await dinner at my family's home in Gibillina, sharing memories of the past and making new ones for my future.

I awaken from the blasting of the horn; the ferry has arrived in Sicily, only 25 minutes across the water. I step off the ferry onto my family's homeland and gaze nostalgically at what has become modern-day Sicily. Little has changed, only I have grown older.

I check into my hotel, and as I sit and write, I put into perspective the reason for writing this book — sharing with you my favorite recipes, all tried and true through the years, new ones and old — and I believe you will treasure them as I have.

Bere mangiare bene!

Jasper's Timeline

1954: Jasper Mirabile starts a small neighborhood bar and restaurant at 75th and Wornall in southern Kansas City.

1959: Jasper completely remodels the neighborhood bar into a grand luxe dining room and lounge and adds a Northern Italian menu and a private dining area.

1967: Jasper purchases the whole block at 75th and Wornall and tears down the buildings and expands the restaurant and the menu into a four-star dining establishment.

1972: Jasper's Restaurant is designated as a Holiday Award Restaurant, a world-wide award, and designated as one of the best restaurants in the world.

1975: Jasper adds a new party room and expands the building with a new lounge and lobby area.

1978: Jasper's becomes a coveted Mobil Four-Star Restaurant "worthy of a special trip."

1981: Jasper totally remodels the restaurant and lounge area to become Kansas City's only grand restaurant.

1984: Jasper's opens Marco Polo's Deli, a small Italian New York-style deli to cater to the desire for fast-paced dining.

1984: Cartier names Jasper's one of the best restaurants in America.

1985: East-West Network names Jasper's one of the top 75 restaurants in America, voted by 100,000 airline frequent flyers.

1989: Jasper's totally remodels the lounge and lobby area and remodels the dining area to enhance the dining experience.

1990: Marco Polo's Deli expands to a trattoria-style restaurant with a casual atmosphere and regional Italian cooking.

1991: Jasper's becomes one of nine Italian restaurants in America to be named worthy of the coveted 4 Diamonds from AAA Motor Club.

1991: Jasper is named to the Board of Directors of both the newly formed Distinguished Restaurants of North America and Gruppo Ristorante Italiano.

1992: Jasper's is named one of the top restaurants in America by the DiRoNA Awards Committee.

1992: Jasper's is named Best of the Best Italian Restaurants in America and awarded Five-Star Diamonds.

1993: Jasper's is the only restaurant in Kansas City to be named worthy of the Mobil 4 Stars, AAA 4 Diamond, the DiRoNA Award and the Gold Five-Star Diamond Award.

1995: Jasper Jr., executive chef, is invited to cook at the James Beard House in New York City. New York food critics give him outstanding reviews. The Beard House is known as the culinary mecca for chefs to showcase their talents.

1996: Jasper, Jr. is again invited to do the James Beard dinner.

1996: Jasper Mirabile, Sr. is voted into the DiRoNA Hall of Fame, one of only 18 other restaurant owners in North America to be so honored.

1997: Jasper's is named as the Best Italian Restaurant in Kansas City by the Zagat Guide.

1998: The Jasper's Restaurant and Marco Polo's buildings are sold to Walgreen Drugs, thus ending 44 years in business. Jasper Sr. retires, and his sons, Leonard and Jasper Jr. purchase the Watts Mill Shopping Center on 103rd and State Line. Plans for a new restaurant, to be open in 1999, are made.

1999: The new Jasper' Restaurant and Marco Polo's Italian Market opens overlooking Watts Mill and Indian Creek.

2000: Jasper's opens a new patio and private dining room, seating an additional 55.

2001: DiRoNA returns our award after a mandatory three-year waiting period, and Leonard is placed on the Board of Directors.

2003: Enoteca da Jasper, Kansas City's first Italian wine bar, opens with over 400 Italian wines and receives rave reviews by local press.

Awards and Recognition

Best Italian Restaurant in Kansas City. .... *Zagat 1998*

Top 10 Italian Restaurants in America. .... *East-West Network*

Distinguished Restaurants of North America Award. .... *since inception of award program*

"Most Satisfying Dish of the Year." .... *USA Today 1999*

Four Stars. .... *Kansas City Star*

Four Diamonds. .... *AAA — Automobile Club of America*

"One of America's Most Honored Restaurants" .... *Bob Lape, WCBS Radio New York*

"A Culinary Delight" — *Rave reviews for the first chef to ever cook at the James Beard House*

Silver Spoon Award .... *Ingram's Magazine*

"The Return of Jasper's Is the Best Gift for Local Gastronomies."
Art Simmering, Kansas City Star food critic

"Jasper's Veal Lemonata Is a Culinary Dream" .... *Craig Claiborne, cookbook author*

"Jasper Jr. is keeping his father's legacy alive with the new Jasper's. The food is memorable."
.... *Charles Ferruzza, noted food critic*

Mobil Four Stars — 25 years. .... *Mobil Travel Guide*

"Best of the Best" .... *Cartier Award*

"Best Italian Restaurant," "Best Chef," "Best Service" .... *The Squire newspaper*

Award of Excellence. .... *Wine Spectator Magazine*

"Traditions come and traditions go; looks like the Mirabiles have a new one going at the new Jasper's" .... *Kansas City Magazine*

"One of America's Top Italian Restaurants." .... *Calvin Trillin, Time Magazine*

"An Italian restaurant in the middle of an oasis" ....
Luige Veronelli , famous Italian food critic

Ambassador 25 Award ....

"Kansas City's only true Italian restaurant" .... *Ford Times Magazine*

"Though Jasper Sr. was born in the United States, his restaurants presented nothing short of authentic cucina" .... *Roberto Donna, noted Italian chef; chairman, Cucina Magazine*

"An Italian Treasure in Kansas City" .... *Bon Appetit*

"Jasper Jr.'s dishes are delightful and inspiring" .... *Midwest Living*

"Kansas City is lucky that Jasper Mirabile, Jr. lives and works in his family's restaurant."
.... *Kansas City Magazine*

"Jasper Mirabile is without doubt, the epitome of a restaurateur."
.... *Robert Lawrence Balzer, L.A. Times food critic*

"Noteworthy Italian dishes" .... *Cucina, Italian Country Journal*

"Top service, top atmosphere, top Italian" .... *Corporate Report Magazine*

The Life of a Restaurateur

A Restaurateur must be a Diplomat, a Democrat, an Autocrat, an Acrobat and a Doormat. He must have the facility to entertain Prime Ministers, Princes of Industry, Pickpockets, Gamblers, Bookmakers, Pirates, Philanthropists, Popsies and Prudes. He must be on both sides of the "Political Fence" and be able to jump the fence.

He should be, or have been, a Footballer, Golfer, Bowler, Tennis Player, Cricketer, Dart Player, Sailor, Pigeon Fancier, Motor Racer and a Linguist, as well as having a good knowledge of any other sport involving Dice, Cards, Horse Racing and Billiards. This is also most useful, as he sometimes has to settle arguments and squabbles. He must be a qualified Boxer, Wrestler, Weight Lifter, Sprinter and Peacemaker.

He must always look immaculate — when drinking with the Ladies and Gentlemen mentioned in the first paragraph, as well as Bankers, Swankers, Theatricals, Commercial Travelers and Company Representatives, even though he has just made peace between any of the two, four, six or more of the aforementioned patrons.

To be successful, he must keep the bar full, the house full, the storeroom full, the wine cellar full, the customers full — and not get full himself. He must have staff who are clean, honest, quick workers, quick thinkers, non-drinkers, mathematicians, technicians, and at all times on the boss' side, the customers' side, and stay on the outside of the bar.

TO SUM UP: *He must be outside, inside, offside, glorified, sanctified, crucified, stupefied, cross-eyes, and if he's not the strong, silent type, there's always suicide!*

— Author Unknown

What Is a Restaurant?

Somewhere between the excitement of the Broadway stage and a September football scrimmage, we find the extraordinary phenomenon called THE RESTAURANT. Restaurants come in assorted sizes, prices and themes. But all restaurants have the same creed: To serve people every minute of every hour of every day.

Restaurants are composite. They are there to fill up, flake out, celebrate and remember. Even forget. To your competition, you are always filled, you are the greatest chef, the cleanest kitchen, and have the best wine list. To your guest, you are a swinger, a party boy, living the life of Riley. And someday, as they always say, "When I retire, I am going to open a place of my own."

Restaurants live with phrases like: "We're two dishwashers short," "The waiter didn't show," "The cook quit," and "What is the count?"

Your customer of 10 years just told you his veal was tough and this is the last time you'll see him.

It's the only business where you are only as good as your last meal ...

A restaurant is a smile on your face with two waiters short. A new tux with tomato sauce on the sleeve. It's shaking hands with the owner of the Chiefs, while your left hand is on the plunger. It's smiling at strangers with only a few hours of sleep, while your sons ask, "When is Dad coming home?"

It's having one son as a lawyer, and one as a doc, two in the business and a wife on the time-clock.

A restaurant is trying to be Cecil B. DeMille and Rodgers and Hart, while the script is written by the bank. It takes the finesse of an art collector with the fortitude and skill of a plumber.

It's 5 p.m. and the sauces are checked, the cooks are late and the bartenders quit. The show must go on, you gather your wits, your back has finally broken, but the curtain has risen.

The bank just called now at 5:30 p.m. The deposit got lost and the accounts are overdrawn. And you holler at the accountant as he screws up the costs, but by now it's 6 p.m. and the show begins.

But ... a restaurant is the Super Bowl, the World Series and Oscar night — all rolled into one when you hear, "It's the best meal I've had ... and we'll be back!"

Thanks, Dad, for being the Director and for teaching us what a restaurant is ...

— Presented to Jasper, Sr. by his son James.

Join Our E-mail List!

By joining our E-mail list, you will receive news, invitations and special offers from Jasper's.

Name _____

E-mail: _____

Your information is safe with us. We will not sell or rent any of your information.

Mail to: Jasper's
             1201 W. 103rd Street
             Kansas City, MO 64114

E-mail to: jasperjr@aol.com

Website: www.jasperskc.com

About the Author

Jasper Mirabile, Jr. was named executive chef of Jasper's in May 1984 at the young age of 22. He had spent the past college years at the University of Nevada, Las Vegas, Hotel and Restaurant School. During summer vacations each year he would travel to Europe to visit cooking schools in Venice, Florence, Sicily and Milan. He was the first chef from Kansas City to be invited to the prestigious James Beard House in New York where he received rave reviews and was recognized by the foundation for

his outstanding efforts and continues to uphold the tradition of authentic Italian cuisine.

Today, Jasper Jr. oversees his kitchen staff, creating regional Italian cuisine and season menus and can be found many nights working the stoves and dining rooms, offering tips to his customers and assistants and preparing new dishes for his guests. Jasper Jr. travels extensively to Italy each year, researching new restaurants, attending cooking classes, wineries and small producers of Italian products.

He currently teaches cooking classes and is working on his second cookbook He is co-chairman of the American Institute of Food and Wine, Convivium leader of Slow Food Kansas City, national board member of Gruppo Ristoratori Italiano.

Please visit his website for more information at:

www.jasperskc.com